Historical Walks
Hong Kong Island

Madeleine H. Tang
Irene Dunning
Ashley H. Baker
Ellen M. Martin

The Guidebook Company

This edition first published in 1988 by The Guidebook Company Limited, The Penthouse, 20 Hollywood Road, Central, Hong Kong.

ISBN 962-217-043-9

Front cover photographs of Government House (residence and office of Hong Kong's Governor), Des Voeux Road, shrine in Paak Sing Ancestral Hall, Canossian Chapel, and window of St John's Cathedral: Ellen M. Martin and Ashley H. Baker

Illustrations and design: Edwin Yu
Maps: Bai Yiliang
Editor: Robyn Flemming

Contents

About the Authors

Madeleine Tang was born in Shanghai and has lived in Hong Kong since 1955. During this time, she has seen Hong Kong develop from a quiet backwater into a leading financial centre in Asia. During that transition, many fine examples of Chinese culture and British colonial monuments were destroyed. Being an avid walker and explorer, Madeleine rediscovered many points of interest hidden away behind the steel and glass of the new Hong Kong. This book was inspired by her combined interests in walking and history.

Irene Dunning was born in Britain, but having lived in Hong Kong for the past 30 years considers herself to be 'Hongkong-ese'. As a result of her dedication to the community life of Hong Kong, she has been actively involved in numerous publications and guided tours in her many fund-raising activities.

Ashley Baker, an American with a Master's Degree in Audiology, worked in New York City for ten years prior to moving to Asia. Ashley, who loves travel and adventure, has lived in Indonesia and Australia and now resides in Hong Kong. During her seven years in Asia, she has led tours, written and published travel articles, and done photography for guidebooks on Indonesia and Australia.

Ellen Martin is an American who has worked as a freelance photographer in the United States and Hong Kong. She lived in Japan, Zimbabwe, and Turkey before moving to Hong Kong. Ellen has walked, backpacked, camped, and studied the history of each of these countries.

Preface

The walks described in this book lead through some of the most historic streets of Hong Kong. They will take the adventurous visitor behind the glass and concrete façade of the modern city into a maze of old-fashioned streets where historic buildings are still to be found and ancient traditions are faithfully observed.

Mrs Madeleine Tang is well known for her invaluable and untiring work for the preservation of the traditional buildings and beautiful country walks of Hong Kong Island and the New Territories.

Now she and her team have carefully planned and researched these unusual city walks which will give pleasure and a deeper understanding of Hong Kong to visitors and residents alike.

Pamela Youde
Wife of the late
Sir Edward Youde
26th Governor of Hong Kong

London

Acknowledgements

Our grateful thanks to Diana Addis and Julia Boyd for their long hours of research; Dr Y.C. Lau, Robyn McLean and staff of the Public Records Office of Hong Kong; Elizabeth Sinn from the University of Hong Kong History Department; E.J.K. Francis, Chief Inspector of the Royal Hong Kong Police Force; Father Dominic Bazzo of the Roman Catholic Cathedral; Mary Wang; Connie Yeung, JT, LD, SB, LM; and the many others who helped, encouraged, and supported us. We are also indebted to the Hong Kong Tramways Ltd, Hong Kong University Press, Oxford University Press, and the published works listed in the bibliography.

Introduction

What is Hong Kong really like? Where is the Hong Kong you have heard about, with rickshaws, junks, temples, and sidewalk markets?

At first glance it may not be obvious, but behind the glossy exterior of this rapidly changing city there still exists an old world with its ancient Chinese culture and respected traditions. Even those of us who live here continue to discover and to be fascinated by the combination of the new and the old that gives Hong Kong its distinctive charm. This is the Hong Kong we would like you to experience.

The best way to see 'old Hong Kong' is on foot. We will lead you back in time through areas seldom seen by most tourists and show you some of the oldest sections of the island where men take their birds for walks and markets sell fresh fish and 100-year-old eggs. Scattered through these areas are small family-operated warehouses where goods have been traded between China and the rest of the world for over 145 years. There are intriguing speciality shops selling Chinese teas and herbs and exotic medicines such as powder of crushed pearl, deer antler, ginseng root, and snake bile.

Since the first settlers arrived, many religions have been practised in Hong Kong. On the walks, you will visit a variety of late 1800–early 1900 houses of worship. It is customary on entering to place a small donation in the offering box.

This book contains five walks between Victoria Peak and Victoria Harbour on the north side of Hong Kong Island, all within a ten-minute taxi ride from the Star Ferry in the Central business district. This northern strip was the first area to be developed by Europeans and is, therefore, most notable for its historical associations.

The name of each walk emphasizes the area where most of the walk is concentrated: **Kennedy Town**, an unlikely name for an area long known for its traditional Chinese herb and medicine shops; **Tai Ping Shan**, known by the British as 'Chinatown' in the early days of the colony; **Mid-Levels**, a residential area settled predominantly by Europeans; **Victoria** (Central), a Western-style commercial district which today bears little resemblance to a colonial city; and **Wanchai Gap**, a wooded area through which an aquaduct once brought water from the south side of the island to Victoria.

Each walk is accompanied by a map. The numbers on the map refer to the sights indicated in the text.

Although this book is predominantly a walking guide, it does incorporate other means of transportation. Walking times vary depending on individual walking speed and the amount of time spent at points of interest, but approximate times are stated at the beginning of each walk. Undoubtedly you have noticed all the hills in Hong Kong, but do not despair, most of the walking is downhill! The walks are independent and can be taken in any order. Chinese characters for the starting point of each walk are appended in case your taxi driver does not recognize the name in English. If at any time you decide to take only part of a walk, remember, you are never more than about a ten-minute taxi ride from the Star Ferry in Central. Now, put on comfortable walking shoes and begin to explore!

Historical Background

Historians tell us that Hong Kong (from the Cantonese 'Heung Gong' meaning 'Fragrant Harbour') was a barren rock inhabited by a few fishermen, farmers, and pirates when the British arrived about 150 years ago. Britain, the leader of Europe's Industrial Revolution, wanted access to the greatest consumer market in the world, China. Her merchants were confined initially to the Portuguese territory of Macau and, during the trading seasons, to Canton, the only Chinese port then open to Europeans. The Chinese government's attempt at restricting British efforts to expand trade became complicated by the issue of opium, first introduced to China by the Portuguese in the 17th and 18th centuries. As opium imports and use increased, the Chinese government found its silver reserves, which had come into China through the export of tea and silk, being depleted to pay for the opium. The opium trade continued despite imperial bans, and as friction over these and other issues intensified, the Opium War broke out in 1839.

At the end of the Opium War in 1842, the Treaty of Nanking was signed between Britain and the defeated Chinese Empire. Among other terms, it broke the Canton monopoly by opening four more ports to foreign trade and provided for the cession of Hong Kong Island to the British. The island was to become a new base for British trade in the East. Situated off the southeast coast of China at the mouth of the Pearl River and having a deep-water port, Hong Kong made an ideal location for the traders to have a safe anchorage and base.

Hong Kong has continued to be one of the most important entrepôts for China, as well as being a major Asia-Pacific trade centre and the largest container port in the world. Today the population of the Territory of Hong Kong, which includes Hong Kong Island, Kowloon, the New Territories, and 235 islands, is approximately 5.5 million. Hong Kong Island is home to almost 1.2 million people. The total land area is 1,070 square kilometres (385 square miles), of which Hong Kong Island accounts for 77.5 square kilometres (30 square miles).

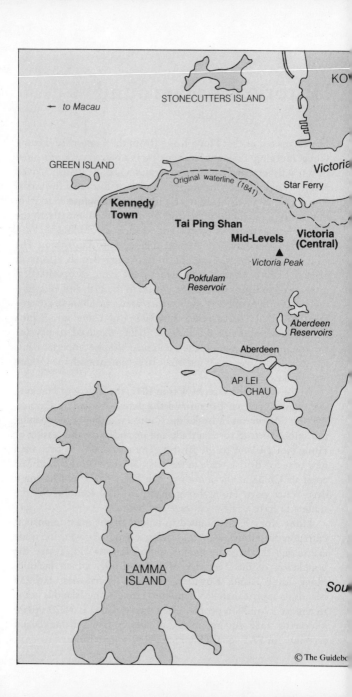

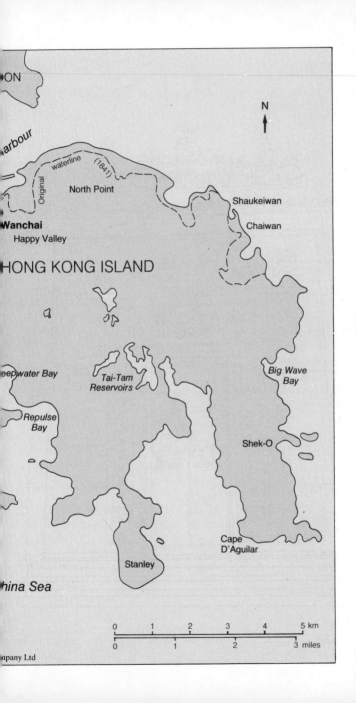

Lu Pan Temple

Kennedy Town

Duration

Approximately 3 hours.

Description

After arriving by taxi or bus at the University of Hong Kong campus, the starting point for the walk, you will travel both on foot and by electric street tram to discover sections of Hong Kong unknown to most tourists. You will visit the university, wend your way down to an isolated temple, and venture into Kennedy Town, one of the most traditional areas of the city.

Points of Interest

Fung Ping Shan Museum (Open: 9.30 am – 6 pm. Closed: Sundays and public holidays), **University of Hong Kong, Lu Pan Temple, Kennedy Town.**

Starting Point

Fung Ping Shan Museum, University of Hong Kong, 94 Bonham Road, Mid-Levels（香港大學馮平山博物館）.

How to Get There

From Kowloon　Take the Star Ferry or the MTR (underground railway) to Central, Hong Kong Island and then follow the directions below.

From Hong Kong Island　Take a taxi to the Fung Ping Shan Museum, or take the No. 3 double-decker bus from the front of the Connaught Centre (the tall building with round windows near the Star Ferry) on Connaught Road. Take some small change for the bus.

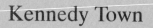

Kennedy Town

Legend

- 🚶 Start walk here
- — Walk line
- 🚌 Car park
- 🚌 Bus stop
- ▥ Steps
- ⛽ Petrol station
- 🚋 Tram stop
- ═ Tram line

| 0 | 50 | 100 | 150 m |
| 0 | 50 | 100 | 150 yds |

Victoria Harbour

Belcher Ga

KENNEDY TOWN PRAYA

SAI CHEUNG ST

HOLLAND STREET

KENNEDY TOWN PRAYA

BELCHER'S STREET

LI PO LUNG

SANDS STREET

CHIN LIN TERR

8

9

PO

KENNEDY TOWN NEW PRAYA

CATCHICK STREET

KENNEDY TOWN

SMITHFIELD STREET

NORTH STREET

TO LI TERRACE

HOK SZ TERRACE

CADOGAN STREET

DAVIS STREET

POKFIELD ROAD

Kennedy Town
Wholesale Market

LUNG WAH STREET

© The Guidebook Company Ltd

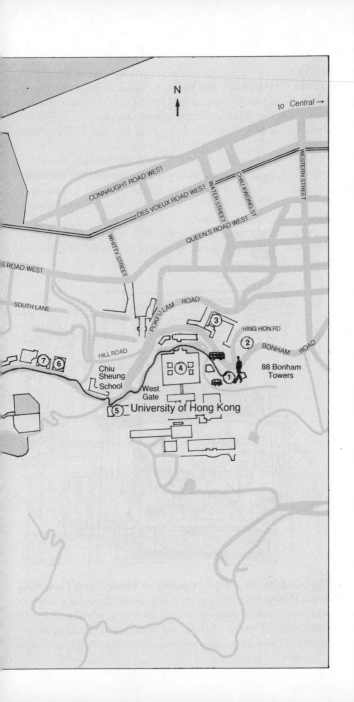

The 10 – 15-minute bus trip takes you up Cotton Tree Drive past the Lower Peak Tram Station to Kennedy Road and Upper Albert Road past Government House. The bus continues along Caine Road to Bonham Road, where you pass the large neo-Gothic-style Hop Yat Church on your left (see Tai Ping Shan Walk, page 30).

Along Bonham Road, look for No. 88 Bonham Towers, a white and green building on your left next to the university grounds, recognizable by a tall Chinese gate and a stone wall with green porcelain bamboo-style struts. This landmark should alert you to prepare to get off at the next stop.

As you alight from the bus, behind you is the university car park exit. Walk back about 45 metres (50 yards) to the Fung Ping Shan Museum.

This walk begins at the **University of Hong Kong Fung Ping Shan Museum** (1), but before going inside, stand for a moment with your back to the museum and look to your right across the street. You will see a delightful **old house** with crumbling yellow plaster (2) framed by banyan trees. This vignette perhaps gives some idea of how **Bonham Road** must have appeared in its heyday before there were cars, when people could stroll in the shade of the banyans enjoying an uninterrupted view across the harbour. Bonham Road was named after Sir Samuel George Bonham, Hong Kong's third Governor (for additional information on Bonham, see pages 29–30).

Now enter the museum, which was built in 1932 with money originally donated by Fung Ping Shan, a prominent Hong Kong businessman, to house the university's library. In 1964 the books were moved to the new library building in the university. Since that time, the premises have been used as a museum. Apart from the excellent temporary exhibitions held here, the museum has a permanent collection of bronzes and ceramics which can be seen on the first and second floors.

The display of bronze mirrors from China's Warring States period (475 – 221 BC) and the large collection of Nestorian crosses are particularly notable. Bronze vessels from various periods are exhibited with photographs clarifying their functions. Also to be seen are seals from the Han period (207 BC – AD 220) and a large bronze drum from the Six Dynasties (220 – 589).

In the ceramics gallery there are some early earthenware pots and an impressive, exceptionally large, Tang Dynasty (618 – 907) camel. There is also a collection of the 18 Disciples of Buddha, made in the early 19th century. These figures were donated by the Fung family, along with many other pieces dating primarily to the Ming (1368 – 1644) and Ch'ing (1644 – 1911) Dynasties.

On leaving the museum, turn left on Bonham Road and left again into the driveway of the university car park. About halfway to the top of the drive, look at **St Paul's College** (3), the modern building on your right across the street. St Paul's was originally founded in 1851. (For a history of St Paul's College, see page 66). As you continue up the hill, passing an information office and a university map on your left, you will see **Loke Yew Hall** (4).

Loke Yew Hall, built in 1912, was originally known as the Great Hall. After the Second World War, this building was extended and renamed for a Malayan Chinese who was a benefactor in the early days of the university. The architecture is striking, particularly in the context of modern Hong Kong, the central part being surmounted by a neo-baroque clock tower and flanked by façades with giant pillars rising through the upper two storeys. The architect was a Mr Bryer of Messrs Leigh and Orange, a leading firm of architects in Hong Kong which is still operating today.

Walk through the vestibule and up the steps. Splinter scars from a shell that landed under the portico during the war can still be seen on some of the granite steps leading to the charming quadrangles of Loke Yew Hall. You can walk around these quadrangles, where the tiled floor and palm trees make a soothing contrast to the noise and bustle of Pokfulam and Bonham Roads outside.

The idea of a university was first suggested as early as 1905 in a *China Mail* editorial, but it was not until 1907, when Sir Frederick Lugard arrived as Governor of the colony, that the project began to get off the ground. At that time the only higher education available was at the College of Medicine (founded in 1887), whose most famous graduate was Dr Sun Yat Sen, the Father of modern China.

Dr Sun Yat Sen was born in 1866 of a peasant family in Kwangtung Province of China. Dr Sun, influenced by the ideas of the Western world, strove for reformation in his homeland and led a revolution which toppled the Manchu Empire in 1911. He established the Chinese Republic and founded the Kuomintang or National People's Party.

There was little enthusiasm for a university in Hong Kong from either the Chinese or the trading community. The Colonial Office in London did not offer any encouragement, dismissively referring to the project as Lugard's 'Pet Lamb'. This did not deter Sir Frederick and Lady Lugard who continued to advocate the founding of a university. They were supported in this by Mr H.N. Mody, a wealthy Parsee businessman, who donated HK$150,000 for the construction and a further HK$30,000 as an endowment. There were many others who, though slow to show interest, became inspired by Sir Frederick and Lady Lugard's enthusiasm and gave generously to the project.

The university opened in 1912 with fewer than a hundred students. In his speech at the opening ceremony, Lugard made the following prophetic observation: 'When the historian of the next century reviews the progress of the Eastern world, it may be that he shall point to this Colony of Hong Kong — a mere speck on the map — as the centre from which emanated an influence which profoundly affected a nation numbering one quarter the population of the world.'

Lugard was not himself a practising Christian and he was adamant that the university should be open to people of all races and creeds, with the stipulation that no one religion should be taught. He also felt it was important that emphasis be placed on subjects of practical benefit, and indeed, leaving aside the already established College of Medicine, the first professor to be installed held the Chair of Engineering. Engineering remained for many years the largest faculty and the only one to award honours degrees. Lack of proper funds was a major problem for the university, but in 1922 some generous help came from America in the form of Rockefeller Institute endowments for establishing three Chairs — in medicine, surgery and obstetrics.

At the very moment the Japanese opened their attack on Hong Kong on 8 December 1941, medical students were taking their final examinations in the Great Hall of the university. Most were subsequently involved in the defence of the colony and a number were killed. However, on New Year's Day 1942, the university authorities, most of whom were by this stage interned in the university, conferred medical degrees, some of them posthumously.

The immediate post-war years were difficult, but today the university has over 8,000 students and more than 500 teachers, the great majority of whom are Chinese. There are now nine faculties.

Turn left out of Loke Yew Hall around the drive which leads to the West Gate. In front of the modern red-brick Haking Wong Building (5), take the foot-bridge over Pokfulam Road and turn right then sharp left and continue until you come to Chiu Sheung School, where you will need to take the pedestrian subway to return to Pokfulam Road. There is now a ten-minute walk which cannot, alas, be described as enticing. Unfortunately there is no other more attractive route to the Lu Pan Temple which is, however, well worth the effort.

Go past the Ho Tung Engineering Workshop (6), dated 1925. During the occupation, the Japanese ransacked and looted all the university's engineering equipment, thus making it impossible to teach engineering degree courses after the war. It was decided, therefore, to offer instead a degree course in architecture, and in 1950 the Duncan Sloss School of Architecture and Engineering (7), named after the then Vice-Chancellor, came into being.

After passing the Duncan Sloss Building at 83 Pokfulam Road, you will come to the William Peel Engineering Laboratories. Shortly afterwards you will see on your right one of the student dormitories, Ricci Hall (8), at 93 Pokfulam Road, named after Matteo Ricci, the famous Jesuit priest who spent much of his life in China in the 16th and early 17th centuries.

About 180 metres (200 yards) from Ricci Hall, look carefully for a flight of steps down the hill to your right. There is a sign with Chinese characters on a red board (魯 班 先 師 廟) pointing the way to the **Lu Pan Temple** (9). (At this point you will see ahead on the left Shell and Mobil petrol stations.) You may, no doubt thankfully, now leave Pokfulam Road. The steps leading down to the Lu Pan Temple are very steep. However, halfway down there is a good excuse for a five-minute rest, for from here there is a superb view of the roof of the temple.

The Lu Pan Temple is set in a broad terrace called Chin Lin (Green Lotus) which, with its banyan trees and shallow steps, is another echo of an older, more leisurely Hong Kong. This temple is the only one in the territory dedicated to Lu Pan and was established in about 1885. (The name 'Lu Pan' does not appear in English on the temple. However, to the left of the main door is a plaque, bearing the name of a Chinese society, which says, 'Kwong Yuet Tong Hong Kong'.)

Lu Pan, the god of carpenters and builders, is said to have been born in 606 BC in the Kingdom of Lu. By the time he was 40, Lu Pan was not only reputed to be the most skilled carpenter of his day, but also to possess miraculous powers. With these powers, he repaired the Pillars of Heaven, the abode of the gods, built a palace for the Queen Mother, and carved magpies which could float for three days in the air. Lu Pan did not die, but merely vanished into the sky, leaving behind only his axe and saw. A feast day is held every year in his honour on the 13th day of the sixth moon of the Chinese calendar, and workers in the construction business come from all over Hong Kong to pay him homage.

This lovely temple has Shih-wan ware along the roof line. Shih-wan pottery was made in kilns which date back to the Ming period, when it was known as five-colour pottery. This hand-made pottery is still being produced today in the area of Shih-wan in China's Kwangtung Province. The temple also has three-dimensional carvings on either side of the main doors. On the doors are painted life-size figures of door gods.

The legend of the door gods dates to the Tang Dynasty (618 – 907) when an emperor and his household were awakened by ghosts and demons banging on the palace doors. The next night, two guards, Ch'in and Yu, were posted outside the doors to scare away the demons. When the demons did not return, the emperor was pleased, but he was concerned that the guards had not slept all night. So he commissioned an artist to paint like-nesses of two fierce armoured men on the doors of the palace. From that time on, this idea was copied and Ch'in and Yu have become the official deities of doorways.

Inside, the temple is serene and inspiring. Again, carvings are found over the doors leading to the incinerator and a small side room. Just inside is a screening door (*dong chung*) which keeps out evil spirits by blocking their path, for evil spirits can only travel in a straight line.

Having seen the temple, continue down the steps which soon turn into a path called Li Po Lung Path. This path, which soon widens into a terrace, passes through a residential quarter which still has some of the flavour of old Hong Kong, with balconies laden with plants, washing strung out of the windows, and chil-dren inventing ingenious games in confined spaces.

You are now in **Kennedy Town**, named for Sir Arthur E. Kennedy under whose governorship (1872–7) this district was first developed. Sir Arthur, a jovial Irishman, was much liked and respected by the local community. According to E.J. Eitel's *Europe in China*, 'It was acknowledged that he had not done much, but he had made himself pleasant to all and his memory was cherished by the Colonists who looked upon him as the Governor who ruled them always with their own consent.'

Kennedy Town came into existence as part of Hong Kong's land reclamation scheme. Most of the labourers hired to work on the scheme had been made redundant as the result of a cut-back in the work-force in the godowns (warehouses) in central

Victoria. With the opening of the Suez Canal in 1869 and the Hong Kong Telegraph in 1871, merchants had quicker access to world markets. Since they no longer needed to maintain large stocks in their godowns, they required less labour.

After a few minutes' walk, the terrace joins **Belcher's Street**, so called after Captain Sir Edward Belcher R.N. (Royal Navy) who surveyed the complicated coastline around Hong Kong, calculated the heights of the main peaks, and is thought to have named them.

Captain Belcher kept a log in which he left the following account of the brief ceremony held at Possession Point, the place where the Union Jack was first hoisted. (Possession Point is in the Tai Ping Shan area. For additional information on this, see Tai Ping Shan Walk, page 33.) 'On the 24th [January 1841] we were directed to proceed to Hong Kong and commence its survey. We landed on Monday the 25th 1841 at 15 minutes past 8 am being the first bonafide possessors. Her Majesty's health was drunk with three cheers on Possession Mount. On the 26th the squadron arrived, the marines landed, the Union [Jack] was hoisted on our post, the formal possession taken of the island, by Commodore Sir J.J.G. Bremer accompanied by the other officers of the squadron, under a *feu-de-joie* from the other marines and a royal salute from the ships of war.'

Cross Belcher's Street at the pedestrian crossing, turn right, and walk one block to Holland Street. Turn left into Holland Street and at the end of the block, turn right and walk a very short distance along **Kennedy Town Praya** until you see the tram stop sign. 'Praya' — a Portuguese-derived word meaning 'waterfront road' — is a reminder of the Portuguese influence in the Canton Delta area.

This walk ends with a leisurely ride on the tram through Kennedy Town. Board the tram at the rear and exit at the front where you pay. The fare is posted and correct change is needed. (At the time of writing, the fare is 60 cents for adults and 20 cents for children under 12.) Trams heading left go west to Kennedy Town Wholesale Market where they turn and travel back to Central District. (An additional fare may be required for the return trip.) The tram follows Kennedy Town Praya, where you may catch a glimpse of an old Chinese junk. Junks were origi-

Loke Yew Hall

nally used for fishing and for transporting goods to and from China. Today, most of them have been replaced by the ships and barges you now see in the harbour.

Hong Kong's harbour, considered to be a very safe and sheltered anchorage, is 52 square kilometres (20 square miles) in area. Long before Captain Charles Elliot landed on the island with a mandate from Lord Palmerston (British Foreign Secretary 1830 – 46) to claim the territory for Britain, there were many small piers and wharves already in existence. Ships from different nations made regular calls at the port to take on fresh water before heading off along the China coast.

It is certainly worth sitting upstairs on the tram, from where you will get one of the best and most exciting views of Hong Kong life in all its diversity. You can either stay on the tram for the 25 – 30-minute ride to Central or wander around Kennedy Town. Kennedy Town is one of the oldest surviving areas of Hong Kong and its atmosphere is like no other!

If you would like to explore this area further, continue on the tram for almost ten minutes to the old centre of trade, sometimes referred to as the Gold Coast area. A good place to leave the tram is 25 Des Voeux Road West. (Refer to Tai Ping Shan map, page 28, for this area.) Cross over Des Voeux Road to where The Hongkong and Shanghai Bank stands and keeping right turn into Ko Shing Street. You are now in **Nam Pak Hong**, meaning 'North-South Trading Houses'. This is an entrepôt area dealing with exotic Chinese specialities — dried shark's fin, bird's nest, abalone, snake, rice, and tea. Most of the native Chinese banks have their origins in this area.

If you decide to stay on the tram to Central, you will soon notice two distinctive red-banded blocks standing like imposing gateways to Hong Kong. One of the blocks houses the Macau Ferry Terminal, rebuilt in 1985.

The Macau Ferry Terminal is operated and managed by the Hong Kong government. A number of commercial companies operate a frequent service to and from Macau, the small Portuguese enclave 64 kilometres (40 miles) to the west of Hong Kong. The journey, depending on weather conditions, takes about three hours by conventional ferry and slightly under one hour by jetfoil.

As the tram turns, on the right stands the red-brick **Western Market,** built in 1858. The tram continues back to Central along **Des Voeux Road,** named after Sir William Des Voeux who served as Governor from 1887 to 1891. You may leave the tram at any stop along the way.

Hong Kong Tramways

In 1881 a bill was introduced to authorize the construction of a tramway 'to be moved by animal, steam or any mechanical power'. However, it was not until 1901 that the Hongkong Tramway Electric Company was formed to operate a route between Kennedy Town (in the west) and Shaukeiwan (in the east). It was another three years before the first tram actually set off at 10 am on 30 July 1904.

Although both European and Chinese residents quickly took advantage of this new mode of transport, some accidents occurred mainly because people failed to appreciate the implications of the tram's fixed path. Out of sheer curiosity, many people would climb on a tram when it stopped, simply to walk through and then get off again, thus causing considerable delays. Legend has it that by passing through the car, a man could shake off any evil spirit following him. Another problem was the gauge of the tracks, which exactly matched that of the numerous two-wheeled carts used to carry goods. The coolies found it much easier to pull their carts along the tracks rather than along the bumpy road surfaces. Later, a similar problem emerged when trucks with the identical wheel gauge also made use of the tram tracks. It seemed the tram tracks were carrying nearly all of Hong Kong's traffic and were, not surprisingly, wearing out much faster than they should have.

In 1912 the first double-decker trams were introduced, but it was not until 1923 that the top decks were given permanent roofs. By 1936 there was a fleet of 97 tramcars, with one passing through the centre of town every 50 seconds. But by the end of the war, the Japanese were operating only 15 trams. With the exception of one major strike and a couple of minor ones since the war, the trams have continued to serve the Hong Kong public faithfully, and they have certainly helped to give the city a distinctive character.

Today, the 164 tramcars carry over 11 million passengers per month along the 36 kilometres (22 miles) of track. In the early days, the tram track followed the shoreline along the harbour, but now that the waterfront has been extended by reclamation, the trams weave between highrise buildings rather than along the harbour.

Emperor Shun Nung (herbalist)

Tai Ping Shan

Duration

Approximately 1½ hours.

Description

This walk takes you through one of the oldest sections of Hong Kong, Tai Ping Shan. You will see the home of the oldest surviving Chinese-Christian group in Hong Kong, the first hospital built by Chinese for Chinese, and two charming secluded Chinese houses of worship and an ancestral hall. You will climb down Ladder Street to the famous Man Mo Temple in the Cat Street – Hollywood Road area, renowned for its antique shops.

Points of Interest

Nethersole Hospital, Hop Yat Church, Tung Wah Hospital Memorial Hall (Open: Weekdays during regular business hours), **Tai Ping Shan, Chinese Temples.**

Starting Point

Nethersole Hospital, 10 Bonham Road, Mid-Levels（般含道邪打素醫院）.

How to Get There

From Kowloon　Take the Star Ferry or the MTR (underground railway) to Central, Hong Kong Island and then follow the directions below.

From Hong Kong Island　Take a taxi to the Nethersole Hospital, a large grey stone building at the junction of Breezy Path and Bonham Road, or take the No. 3 double-decker bus from the front of the Connaught Centre (the tall building with round windows) on Connaught Road. Take some change for the bus.

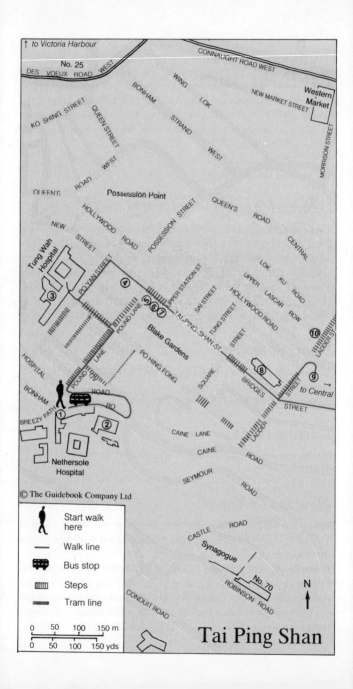

↑ to Victoria Harbour

CONNAUGHT ROAD WEST

No. 25
DES VOEUX ROAD WEST

Western Market

BONHAM STRAND WEST
WING LOK
NEW MARKET STREET
KO SHING STREET
QUEEN STREET WEST
MORRISON STREET

QUEEN'S ROAD WEST

Possession Point

QUEEN'S ROAD CENTRAL

HOLLYWOOD ROAD
POSSESSION STREET
NEW STREET

Tung Wah Hospital
③
PO YAN STREET
④
⑤⑥⑦
POUND LANE
Blake Gardens
UPPER STATION ST
TAI·PING·SHAN·ST
SAI STREET
TUNG STREET

LOK KU ROAD
UPPER LASCAR ROW
HOLLYWOOD ROAD
⑩
LADDER ST

HOSPITAL PATH
POUND LANE
PO HING FONG
SQUARE
BRIDGES STREET
⑧
⑨ to Central

BREEZY PATH
BONHAM ROAD
BO
①
②
CAINE LANE
LADDER ROAD
CAINE ROAD

Nethersole Hospital

SEYMOUR ROAD

© The Guidebook Company Ltd

CASTLE ROAD

Synagogue
No. 70
ROBINSON ROAD

N
↑

🚶	Start walk here
—	Walk line
🚌	Bus stop
▥	Steps
═	Tram line

0   50   100   150 m
0   50   100   150 yds

CONDUIT ROAD

Tai Ping Shan

The ten-minute bus trip takes you up Cotton Tree Drive past the Lower Peak Tram Station to Kennedy Road and Upper Albert Road past Government House. The bus continues along Caine Road to Bonham Road, where you pass the large neo-Gothic-style Hop Yat Church on your left. At this point, press the bell to stop the bus at the next stop, which is in front of the Nethersole Hospital.

Sixty-year-cycle gods (Tai Sui)

The Alice Ho Miu Ling **Nethersole Hospital** (1) marks the beginning of this walk. In order to get a better look at the hospital, cross Bonham Road and enter the Bonham Road Rest Garden. The history of the Nethersole Hospital is discussed below in conjunction with the Hop Yat Church. Also from this point, look across at the Breezy Path and Bonham Road junction, where you can still see a few terraced houses with old colonial shutters.

Bonham Road was named for Hong Kong's third Governor, Sir Samuel George Bonham (governed 1848 – 54), who succeeded Sir John Davis. Bonham served in the East India Company and became the Governor of the Straits Settlements before being selected as Governor of Hong Kong, Plenipotentiary and Superintendent of Trade in China. He was knighted in 1851 and became a baronet in 1852.

Bonham arrived in Hong Kong in 1848 at a very early stage of the colony's development. The cost to the British of administering this newly acquired outpost was far higher than anticipated, particularly as the island's performance as a trading port was initially disappointing. This was largely because much of the China trade, instead of coming through Hong Kong, went through the Treaty Ports (Foochow, Amoy, Shanghai, Ningpo, and Canton) which were opened under the Treaty of Nanking (1842). In spite of the difficult conditions during his term of office, however, Bonham was miraculously able to solve many of the colony's financial problems without having to resort to further taxation on the community, making him both a successful and popular governor.

During his tenure, a bi-monthly mail service between Hong Kong and Europe was established; Hong Kong was elevated to the status of Bishop's See and Diocese of the Church of England; and leases on land were extended to 999 years.

In 1851 a fire in a wooden clothier shop swept through the Western District and destroyed over 400 Chinese houses. During rebuilding, new streets were laid and new houses were constructed of stone and brick. It was decided to fill in a creek with debris from the fire, and Hong Kong's first land reclamation became a road subsequently called Bonham Strand after Sir Samuel George Bonham.

Leave the park, turn left and walk about 45 metres (50 yards) along Bonham Road to the Hospital Road intersection. To the right across the street you will see a neo-Gothic church of brick and stucco painted cream with brown trim. This bold, imposing building at 2 Bonham Road is the **Hop Yat Church** (2), built in 1925 and home of the oldest surviving Chinese-Christian group in Hong Kong.

The church was founded by Dr James Legge, a preacher, educator, and Sinologue (a specialist in the study of Chinese, especially language, literature, history, and culture). He was one of the earliest protestant missionaries to come to Hong Kong, arriving in 1843 from Malacca with nine converts who formed the nucleus of the reorganized Anglo-Chinese College which was originally founded in Malacca in 1819. But he is probably best known for his translations of Chinese classics, in particular the works of Confucius.

In around 1844, Legge organized a Union Church for services both in Chinese and English. Later, as a fully independent congregation, the worshippers adopted the name To Tsai Church. In about 1926, they moved from Hollywood Road to the present site on Bonham Road, renaming their new church Hop Yat Church, and bringing the cornerstone from the old church to incorporate into the new building. This cornerstone is located on the right side outside the main entrance.

A former pastor of the church was named Ho Fuk Tong. One of his sons, Ho Kai, went to England to study law and medicine. There he married an Englishwoman named Alice Walkden, who died of typhoid fever two years after her arrival in Hong Kong. Her bereaved husband channelled his grief into good works by endowing the Alice Memorial Hospital (1887) and the Alice Maternity Hospital (1904). The first training course for general nursing ever held in South China was established with the opening of the Alice Maternity Hospital. Ho's sister, Ho Miu Ling (wife of the first Chinese to be admitted as a barrister to the Hong Kong Supreme Court and the first Chinese appointed to the Legislative Council), also gave money for a new hospital. Built at Breezy Path on government-donated land in 1906, this was the Ho Miu Kwai Hospital. These three hospitals, together with the Nethersole Hospital endowed by businessman W.H. Davis in memory of his mother, were run by the London Mission Society. Today, all four hospitals are under one roof in Bonham Road as the Alice Ho Miu Ling Nethersole Hospital.

Ho Kai's name is perhaps better remembered in connection with Hong Kong's airport. Together with his friend Au Tak, owner of a well-known photographic store, he formed a company to develop land which later became the site of Hong Kong's international airport, Kai Tak.

Turn left down Hospital Road for about a block until you reach some steps leading down into **Pound Lane**. Go down these steps. According to the Jarrett Papers in the Government Public Records Office, this street is thought to be so named because a government pound for animals was located in this area. It is also believed that cattle wandered freely here.

Continue down Pound Lane for a short distance until you come to Po Hing Fong Street (Precious Celebration Street). Turn left here. Ahead you will see a tall white building with Chinese characters. This is the **Tung Wah Hospital** (3) and the inscription marks the centennial of its foundation.

The Tung Wah Hospital was the first hospital in Hong Kong to be run by the Chinese for the Chinese. Before its opening in 1872, sick and dying Chinese who were poor had nowhere to go. More often than not, they were left in the Kwong Fuk T'sz on nearby Tai Ping Shan Street (see below). Discovery of this sort of 'death' house in 1869 provoked an outcry from government officials and a few prominent members of the Chinese community, which led to the establishment of Tung Wah Hospital.

The Chinese community donated HK$30,000 and the sixth Governor, Sir Richard Macdonnell, provided an additional HK$115,000 in the form of a grant to establish this first Chinese hospital. The original building stood across the street from the present hospital.

The Tung Wah Group of Hospitals later branched into other charitable activities. It opened a free school for the poor in 1880, next to the Man Mo Temple. It provided repatriation of refugees, homes for the homeless, and relief for natural disaster victims. It also provided free coffins and burials. When there was a sharp rise in food costs in 1919, Tung Wah set up rice stations for the distribution of free meals. It also established shops for inexpensive commodities. In 1922 a school of Western nursing was opened by the Tung Wah Group.

Today, apart from the hospitals, the directors of the Tung Wah Group of Hospitals are still responsible for coffin houses (a place for storing coffins until the bodies can be taken back to their native village for burial), cemeteries, old people's homes, funeral parlours, temples, youth centres, day nurseries, and schools and colleges.

Walk towards the hospital down a series of steps on Po Hing Fong Street. Cross Po Yan Street (Precious Gratitude Street), which until 1870 was named Fan Mo Street (Grave Street), and enter the hospital area via the driveway. Go in the first door on the right and walk past some stairs into the quadrangle. Turn right at the first door which leads into the large **Ceremonial**

Hall. High above the altar hangs a golden plaque, one of two presented to the Tung Wah Hospital by Emperor Kuang-Hsü of the Ch'ing Dynasty in appreciation of a donation to the China relief fund by the Tung Wah. The second plaque now hangs in the Man Mo Temple.

On the wall behind the altar is a framed picture of Emperor Shun Nung, the famous herbalist. On either side are two floor-to-ceiling black plaques with classical Chinese gold characters which date to Kuang-Hsü (1875 – 1908). These commemorate the opening of the hospital. On the right as you face the altar, at the top-most section of the wall, are photographs, one of which is of Sir Richard Macdonnell surrounded by the founders of the Tung Wah. The other photographs are of benefactors of the hospital. All around the room hang other memorial and testimonial plaques. The lovely old Chinese furniture is made of blackwood.

Retrace your steps until you are standing in front of the hospital, then turn left and continue down Po Yan Street for about a block. Enter the second street on the right, **Tai Ping Shan Street**, which gave its name to this district.

Tai Ping Shan, which means 'Peaceful Mountain', is one of the oldest parts of the city. This quarter of Hong Kong is one of several administrative districts into which Victoria was divided in about 1857. For many years, Tai Ping Shan was referred to as 'Chinatown' because it was one of the three areas where the Chinese lived after the arrival of the British.

Not far from here was the spot where the British first planted the Union Jack in 1841. Modern development has overtaken what was once **Possession Point**, and unfortunately there is nothing left today to mark this historic site.

The following description of Tai Ping Shan by a sanitation engineer named Chadwick gives an idea of how it appeared in 1880: '...in the rear is the densely packed Chinese quarter. This portion of about 1 mile...may be said to be the heart of the town. In front of it are anchored seafaring and river steamers of all sizes, sailing vessels and junks whilst moored alongside the wharf is a dense mass of boats and barges. The streets running up the slopes of the hill at right angles to the shore line are far too steep for wheeled vehicles....'

Conditions became overcrowded and squalid in this area of tightly packed, steeply pitched dwellings. People lived mostly in matsheds, which were houses made of bamboo frames, palm leaf walls, and thatched roofs. These matsheds were breeding places for mosquitoes and rats. Sanitation was a constant problem, and diseases such as typhoid, typhus, and cholera were prevalent. Successive governors made attempts at improving the area but were always distracted by other events in the colony.

Some of the problems that faced the governors were pirates, police corruption, and illegal gambling houses — many of which were located in the Tai Ping Shan area. As early as the 1850s, Sir John Bowring (the fourth Governor of Hong Kong) had sug gested licensing some of these gambling houses because constables were taking bribes anyway. The Victorian government in London turned down the proposal. Between 1867 and 1872, appeals were again made, and at these times some licences were granted.

Apparently governed by the Triads, Tai Ping Shan was a part of the island to which Europeans did not venture. The term 'Triad Society', originally a political and religious organization, is now used for all Chinese secret societies.

'The term "Triad" is an English designation for the sacred symbol of the society: a triangle enclosing a secret sign derived from the Chinese character *hùng* (洪). The resulting sign (洪) has no meaning in itself, but when enclosed by the triangle thus (洪) it is symbolic of the union of Heaven, Earth and Man, the three intersecting microcosms of the universe.' (Ho Fuk-Cheung for the Royal Asiatic Society, see Bibliography.)

Conditions did not improve and when a major plague broke out in 1894, this was the area where it took the most lives. Several hundred troops were brought in to move the sick to temporary hospitals. The government recalled half of the troops after some of their number contracted the plague.

'There was deep Chinese prejudice against Western medicine, and against government interference and intrusion upon their privacy, and much complaint against the house-to-house visitation.... The Tung Wah made strong representations to take over completely the treatment of Chinese victims, but Robinson [Hong Kong's fifth Governor] refused to give in. Placards appeared in Canton, warning Chinese women against going to the colony... thousands fled to the mainland. 109 plague-stricken bodies were collected in one day in June; 350 houses were condemned, 7,000 Chinese were dislodged from their homes, and much of the Tai Ping Shan district was cordoned off or closed.' (G.B. Endacott, *A History of Hong Kong.*) The plague continued to be a problem in the colony until the mid-1920s.

To the right, on a hill just a short distance before the junction with Pound Lane, you will see the first of three traditional houses of worship, **Paak Sing (Kwong Fuk T'sz)** (4). This is the site of the original Kwong Fuk T'sz, which dates from 1851 when a group of local people established it as the 'Wide Blessings Public Ancestral Hall' to hold the ancestral tablets of Chinese expatriates who died while away from their native villages. It became a place to store encoffined bodies awaiting return to mainland China, as well as a place to leave the sick and dying. Paak Sing ('hundred surnames') means that, unlike most ancestral halls, this hall was not restricted to the dead of one family or clan.

The existing hall was rebuilt in 1895 after the plague caused the clearance of much of this area. Today, it is a public Ancestral Hall where, for an initial fee of HK$600 and additional annual offerings, you can have the name of your dead relative inscribed on a tablet. Ancestral tablets are usually small pieces of wood, about 30 by 7.5 centimetres (12 by 3 inches), on which appear the name and birthdate of the deceased.

As you climb the stairs, at a point a few steps from the top, you will see a small open area for devotion, where worshippers believe the soul passes on its journey to the life after death. On the offering table stands a stone White Tiger, which is worshipped for protection against misfortune. Behind this area is a shrine to the Monkey God, who is believed to be able to cure sickness. Known as the 'Great Sage Equal to Heaven', he appeals to the rebellious, mischievous side of man.

As you enter the hall, you will see a bell on the right and some steps on the left leading to a little room filled with old commemorative tablets with pictures honouring the dead.

Standing on the main red carved altar, with its offerings of oranges, tea, and sweets, is a statue of Dei Zhong Wang, who is associated with the worship of ancestors and Yin and Yang. Yin and Yang are male and female forces in Chinese cosmology from which all things are created and balanced, resulting in harmony.

Pass behind the altar and through to a courtyard where there is an incinerator for burning paper offerings. Enter the back room, which houses more ancestral tablets and photographs of the dead. These are so blackened by age and smoke that it is difficult to see if the frames still hold pictures of those commemorated.

As you leave Paak Sing, turn right. On the right-hand corner at the junction with Pound Lane is a small red ceramic shrine to an **Earth God** (T'u Ti) (5). Earth Gods have been worshipped in China, on the 2nd and 16th of every month by the lunar calendar, for thousands of years. Their beginnings can be traced to animism during the Neolithic Age. They are believed to protect small communities and to rule over neighbourhoods. The T'u Ti listens to local rumours, and is the registrar of local events. Usually, shrines to Earth Gods are placed in the open. Images of other gods may also be found and worshipped in the same shrine.

Climb the steps of Tai Ping Shan Street and explore the two temples on your right. The first, the **Sui Tsing Paak Temple** (6) at 38 Tai Ping Shan Street, is fronted with green tiles shaped like bamboo. The temple may have been established as early as the 1894 plague or as late as 1901. Sui Tsing Paak (which means 'Pacifying General') was a nobleman whose name was Chan. Because he is worshipped as one who possesses the power to cure sickness, the residents of Tai Ping Shan brought his image to Hong Kong from China in the hope of suppressing the plague of 1894.

The smell of incense coils hanging in spirals from the roof greets you as you enter the front room, or veranda. The strips of red paper hanging on the coils are printed with prayers expressing either requests or thanks. Each coil will burn for several weeks to ensure that the gods have sufficient time to absorb the prayers. At the far end of the room is a shrine to Kuan Yin, Goddess of Mercy.

Leading off the veranda are two other rooms. The one on the left is the Main Hall of the Temple, and the other houses fortune tellers. In the Main Hall in front of the altar is a glass case containing the statue of 'the Pacifying General'. On the altar is Chai Kung, one of the Buddhas. Not too long ago, Chai Kung was brought here from a temple in Wanchai, so today this temple is also referred to as the Chai Kung Temple. This room also houses the 60 gods (Tai Sui), each of which is dedicated to one specific year in the 60-year cycle in the Chinese calendar. In order to avert calamity, worshippers make an offering to the image corresponding to the year of birth. It is interesting to note that the parents of a newborn child pray to the god of the first year, since the Chinese believe that babies are aged one at birth.

Next door at No. 36 is **Kuan Yin Temple** (7), which was relocated from the waterfront in 1894. It has a very charming wrought-iron front, shaped as lotus plants and flowers. Lotus is the floral symbol of Buddhism, representing the growth of beauty out of mud and stagnant water and symbolizing the hope that anyone can attain enlightenment no matter how downtrodden they may be. The temple is dedicated to the 'Goddess of Mercy', the 'Hearer of Cries', who is particularly important to women in helping with domestic troubles, infertility, and sick or problem children.

The Goddess of Mercy was named Miao Chung (Miao Shan). She was said to be the daughter of a king, and is the Chinese equivalent of India's Avalokitsvara. There are many variations on the legend of how she became the Goddess of Mercy, but they all essentially hold that she refused to marry because she wanted to devote her life to reducing the unhappiness and suffering of mankind and to making all people equal. Her father was said to have been so furious that she fled to a safe fortress. However, she was discovered and slain. Later, because of her purity in life, she was transformed into a goddess. Kuan Yin is worshipped by women in China on the 19th day of the second, sixth, and ninth moons. Worshippers pray for children (particularly sons), wealth, and protection against misfortune. Kuan Yin is generous with her favours and shows great compassion towards those who commit sins in ignorance.

There is an altar table with a gold-painted carved base in the Main Hall. Lovely brass oil lamps sit on this table and hang above it. Beautifully polished brass incense holders stand near the main shrine, and on the wall just to the right hang small braided prayer rugs.

The image of Kuan Yin is enshrined here, along with other popular gods. This image is said to have been carved from wood found in the sea in 1840 by the wife of one of the founders of the temple.

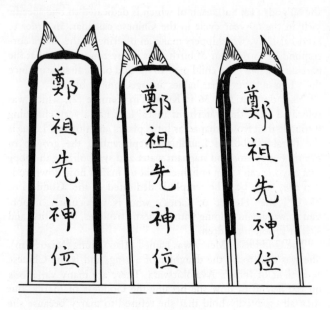

Ancestral tablets

After visiting the temples, turn right and continue along Tai Ping Shan Street (away from Pound Lane). Cross Square Street and go up the steps to **Bridges Street**. Bridges Street was named for an infamous barrister, Dr W.T. Bridges, who made a fortune not only through his private legal practice and money-lending but also in opium dealing. He was Acting Attorney General and Acting Colonial Secretary between 1848 and 1859. To the left is a substantial red-brick building, one of the original **YMCAs** (8).

At the end of the 19th century, some interest was expressed in opening a YMCA in Hong Kong. In 1901, rooms for the Chinese YMCA opened in Des Voeux Road. These premises were inadequate, and it later moved to 34 Queen's Road Central (where the King's Theatre now stands). On 9 March 1912, Lord Lugard laid the foundation stone for a new hostel on Bridges Street, and the building was occupied in March 1913. Later, additional space was needed and a new YMCA was built just opposite the students' hostel on Bridges Street. It opened in

October 1918 and continues to serve the busy community around it.

At the far side of the YMCA runs **Ladder Street**, so named because of its almost vertical arrangement of steps. Ladder Street was built as a path for sedan chair bearers to carry people and cargo up to Mid-Levels. Along its edges are still some old-style houses with balconies and shutters.

Walk down these steps to **Man Mo Temple** (9) at the Hollywood Road intersection. This temple is run by the Tung Wah Group of Hospitals. Donations are used mainly for temple upkeep.

Man Mo Temple was built on one of the narrow dirt paths winding up to Victoria Peak in about 1842, when Hong Kong was founded. Most of the traditional temples contain smoke towers, bell towers, and a Main Hall, and the Man Mo is no exception. The altars, brassware, and pewter were made in China and shipped to Hong Kong over 100 years ago.

Man Mo means 'civil' and 'martial', and the temple is dedicated to two gods: Man Cheong, the God of Civil Servants and Literature, and Kwan Kung, the red-faced God of War. Kwan Kung was a famous warrior who was captured during battle. He was beheaded when he refused to reveal secret plans. He personifies all the virtues of a warrior and a knight and is worshipped by both Buddhists and Taoists. He is a patron of the military, pawn shops, curio dealers, restaurants, and certain aspects of wealth. All brotherhoods, secret societies, and the Police Force look to him as a guardian. It is interesting to note that he is also worshipped by rogues and thieves!

Enter the temple through the door on your left. Just inside is a red carved *dong chung*, a screen which blocks the path of demons and evil spirits who can travel only in straight lines. To the left are two glass cases containing three antique divine chairs dating back to between 1847 and 1885. These chairs were used during festivals to carry the statues of Man and Mo.

Opposite the chairs are a drum and a temple bell, which was cast in 1847 in China. The sounding of the bell and drum usually marks ceremonies and the giving of offerings. The noise is also believed to summon the gods and scare away evil spirits.

On the other side of the *dong chung* is the smoke tower filled with incense coils. These coils are long-burning offerings for prayers of health, success in business, or happiness. Lining this smoke tower on two sides are tall poles with brass symbols of the Eight Immortals, made in 1880. It is believed that they achieved immortality during the Yuan Dynasty (1279 – 1368). Each of the Immortals represents a different condition of life and is credited with special magical powers. In this same area are two three-legged incinerators where paper offerings are burned, and two large brass incense containers.

On the marble-topped table between the smoke tower and the Main Hall are two solid brass deer, symbols of long life. On a similar table in front of the altar are five pewter ritual vessels.

The main altar and the two altars either side are about four and a half metres (15 feet) high and were carved during the Ch'ing Dynasty (1644 – 1911). The gods on the main altar are Man and Mo. Man is on the right in a red robe. In front of him stands a pole with a brass hand holding a pen. Mo is on the left, in green. He wears the imperial head-dress and in front of him is the executioner's sword which symbolizes his own death. A magistrate would go to the temple to worship Mo after an execution so that the spirit of the criminal did not haunt him.

The God of Justice, on the left altar, is dedicated to Pau Kung. Pau always wears black robes. The City God on the right altar is dedicated to Shing Wong. His job is to ensure that everyone gets his just reward, either while living or in the life after death. He is the guardian of city dwellers and when they die he speaks to the ten judges who arbitrate on the sins of the deceased and hand out punishment.

Leave the Main Hall, turn left, and enter the hall of fortune tellers. This hall is called Litt Shing Kung or All Saints Temple.

When you leave the Man Mo Temple, you will be on **Holly-wood Road**. In the 1850s much of this area was woodland, rocky bluffs, and ravines. When the road was built, Hong Kong's second governor, Sir John Davis, named it nostalgically after his English country residence, Hollywood Towers. Today, Hollywood Road is a fascinating thoroughfare known for its Asian antiques, curios, and artifacts.

Another intriguing street in this area (to the front and left of the Man Mo Temple) is Upper Lascar Row, commonly known as **'Cat Street'** (10). 'Cat Street' was actually two streets, Upper and Lower Lascar Row, which were linked together by Ladder

Street. The name 'Lascar', meaning 'East Indian sailor', was probably given to these roads because it was the area where the East Indian sailors lived between voyages.

There are many explanations about the origin of the name 'Cat Street'. Some say it was a red-light district with many 'cathouses'. Others say it was a 'thieves market' which attracted the stolen goods of 'cat burglars'. While still others believe it was derived from the Pidgin English cry of the pedlars, 'Catchee', meaning 'to buy'. Today the lanes of 'Cat Street' are filled with bric-à-brac and both fake and real antiques.

At this point, the Tai Ping Shan Walk comes to an end. This is a wonderful area to explore, so you may want to venture down into 'Cat Street' or stroll along Hollywood Road. If not, you can take a taxi or continue walking to Central.

If you want to walk to Central, it is a ten-minute walk through several interesting market streets. With the Man Mo Temple at your back, turn right on Hollywood Road and follow it to Peel Street. (See Mid-Levels map, pages 44–5, for this area.) Turn left into Peel Street and walk down through the stalls specializing in Chinese-style ladies clothing. Behind a series of stalls are several shops selling items for religious offerings. Turn right at Wellington Street and at the next corner turn left into Graham Street. All along Graham Street is a sidewalk market selling such things as fresh fruits, vegetables, meat, fish, rice, and 100-year-old eggs. Graham Street leads into Queen's Road Central across from the Central Market.

陸羽茶室

LUK YU TEA HOUSE

Luk Yu Teahouse

Mid-Levels

Duration

Approximately 1¾ hours.

Description

Once you have reached the starting point by bus or taxi, you will travel by foot through areas with different styles of religious architecture — Jewish, Muslim, Catholic, and Chinese. Take a tantalizing glimpse at old works of Chinese art. Visit the oldest police compound in Hong Kong, sample tea from China, and stand on a spot that was once part of Victoria Harbour.

Points of Interest

Synagogue, Mosque, Catholic Mission, Chinese Shrine, Central Police Station, Traditional Chinese Teahouse.

Starting Point

Ohel Leah Synagogue, 70 Robinson Road, Mid-Levels.
（ 羅便臣道猶太會 ）

How to Get There

From Kowloon   Take the Star Ferry or the MTR (underground railway) to Central, Hong Kong Island and then follow the directions below.

From Hong Kong Island   Take a taxi to 70 Robinson Road, or take the No. 12 bus from the front of the Connaught Centre (the tall building with round windows) on Connaught Road. You will need some small change for the bus fare.

The bus takes you through Central District to Seymour Road where it starts an uphill climb. Get off at the top of the hill where Seymour joins Robinson Road. At this point you can see

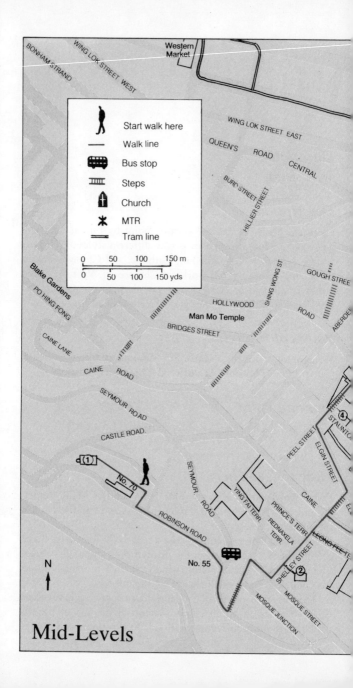

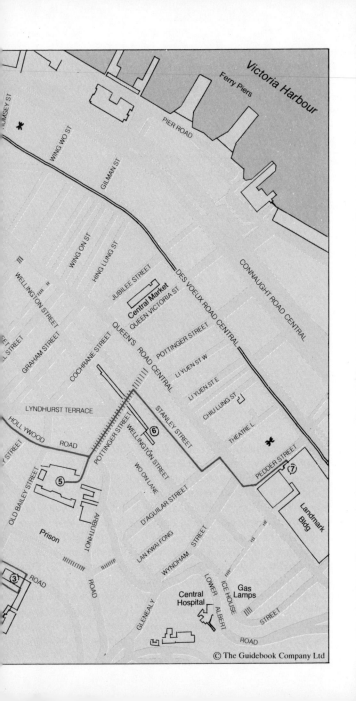

Palm Court, 55 Robinson Road, across from the bus stop. Cross into Robinson Road and continue along past a small police box until you reach 70 Robinson Road.

Ohel Leah Synagogue

This walk begins in a section of town called Mid-Levels, a strip of hillside halfway between Victoria Harbour and Victoria Peak. You will start with a look at the Jewish Synagogue at No. 70 Robinson Road. Unfortunately, at the time of publication, the fate of Hong Kong's only synagogue is unknown because of a controversial redevelopment proposal. Walk down the driveway leading to the synagogue and you will see on your left the Jewish Recreation Club. Walk left past this building and cross over the courtyard through the double gates into the grounds of **Ohel Leah Synagogue** (1). Jewish community life began in Hong Kong in the late 1850s. The synagogue services were held in a variety of temporary buildings until Mr D.H. Silas, with the support of a number of other interested people, finally obtained the site on which the present synagogue stands. The building is one of only two known Sephardic-style synagogues still existing in the Far East.

Sir Jacob E. Sassoon and his brothers provided the funds to build the synagogue in honour of their mother, Lea Gubbay Sassoon. Construction started on 1 May 1878, but the building was not completed until 1902. The Sassoon family in Hong Kong dates back to the beginning of the colony when it was involved in Hong Kong's early trade. The adjoining Recreation Club was donated in 1901 by another prominent member of the community, Sir E. Kadoorie.

As you leave 70 Robinson Road, turn left and continue along Robinson Road, past Seymour Road, until you see a long set of steps going down on your left. Take these steps down past Mosque Junction to Mosque Street. (On the corner is a yellow fire hydrant and a garage with No. 28 over the door.) Turn right.

Turn left at the next corner, which is Shelley Street. (There is a small grocery-type store on this corner, marked 31 Shelley Street.) A few metres along on your right is the entrance to **Jamia (Mohammedan) Mosque** (2). The mosque is open to the faithful on Fridays only. The building opposite the entrance to the mosque is a hostel offering free accommodation to people of the Moslem faith passing through Hong Kong.

In 1850, with the growth of the Mohammedan community, a movement was started to have a mosque built. The first mosque was built in the mid-1850s on the site where the present mosque now stands. Over the years, the congregation increased and in 1915 Mr H.M.H. Esack Elias, from Bombay, donated private funds to rebuild the mosque on the original site. The foundation stone was laid on 15 August 1915.

On leaving the grounds, turn right into Shelley Street. On the way down, if you look to your left, you will see **Rednaxela Terrace**. At first glance, the name is reminiscent of an old Roman name until you realize that it is 'Alexander' spelled backwards, probably a misspelling of Queen Alexandra's name!

Another point of interest on the way down is the rather charming Leong Fee Terrace on your right. If you turn into this terrace and walk along through the gate into a garden courtyard, you will find an excellent view of the Canossian Chapel (see below).

Walk back to Shelley Street and continue until you reach two sets of steps. You will come back later to the steps on the left. Take the few steps down on the right and turn right into Caine Road. After a short walk along the road, there is a high stone wall on your right, where you will see the original gateway to the Sacred Heart Canossian College which was built in 1860 and is now known as the **Canossian Missions** (3). The entrance to the mission is about 50 metres (55 yards) along at 26 Caine Road. After checking with the receptionist for permission to view the chapel, walk up the driveway into the grounds. It is so quiet and peaceful here that you will feel as though you have left Hong Kong. Before taking the steps on the left to the chapel, look across at the Memorial Square, dedicated to the first Canossian missionaries. It is a very pleasant place to sit for a while to absorb the atmosphere.

Early on, the mission established a number of small schools which provided the Portuguese community with an English education. Many Portuguese settlers lived in the Shelley Street area until about the 1860s when they moved to Kowloon. They were employed mainly by the Hong Kong government and the big merchant *hongs* as clerks, accountants, and shroffs.

The term 'hong' was used in China as far back as the late 1500s for commercial firms engaged in trade with foreign countries. Many of those original trading houses, such as Jardine, Swire, Wharf, and Hutchison, still do business in Hong Kong today. A 'shroff' is a Far Eastern native expert employed to test coins and detect counterfeits. Use of the word seems now to be confined to Hong Kong.

The Canossian Sisters (Daughters of Charity) were founded by Magdalene, the Marchioness of Canossia, at Verona, Italy. In 1859 the Prefect Apostolic, Father Aloysius Ambrosi, wrote to Rome requesting the help of the Canossian Sisters in educating the women of his parish. Father Ambrosi believed that women had a right to be educated in order to raise them from their indolent existence.

While waiting for a reply to his request, he enlisted the services of Miss Emily Bowring, a devout Catholic, to help him in his cause. She was the youngest daughter of Sir John Bowring, fourth Governor of Hong Kong (1854 – 9). When Sir John left Hong Kong in April 1859, Emily decided to remain behind and dedicate her life to the church.

On 12 April 1860, six Sisters of the Canossian Order arrived in Hong Kong, where an unfurnished house was rented for them. Upon their arrival, and before taking them to their own house, one of the Catholic Fathers escorted the Sisters to the home of Mr and Mrs Leo D'Almada e Castro, where they met Miss Emily Bowring. Within a short time she had become their first novice, taking the name of Sister Aloysia when she took the veil two years later.

Within two weeks of landing in Hong Kong, the Sisters had 60 girls in their care. Their commitment to the church and teaching, combined with a renewed interest in education by many of the non-Catholic British civil servants in the colony, created a need for much larger premises.

The generous Mr D'Almada e Castro came to their aid by donating a plot of land close to the Sisters' 'Little House', which was known as the Canossian Convent. Construction began in 1860, and by June 1861 the spacious new convent was completed. It had a small chapel, Sisters' quarters, and accommodation for pupils, orphans, and babies, as well as a number of large airy rooms for day-scholars. The present Convent Chapel was built in 1907.

Retrace your steps along Caine Road to Shelley Street. Take the steps up to the footbridge and cross over Caine Road. Continue on Shelley Street, then turn left into Elgin Street, and right into Peel Street. This is an area which has many printing companies and porcelain-ware exporters. Cross Staunton Street, but before descending the steps into Peel Street, have a look at the small shrine on your right which is dedicated to the **City God** (4) of the district.

The City God is the guardian of city dwellers. He ensures that everyone gets his just reward, either in this life or in the life after death. When someone dies, the City God speaks on his behalf to the ten judges who wait to judge the sins of the deceased and to hand out punishment.

Continue walking down until you come to Hollywood Road, famous for its many antique shops. Turn right into Hollywood Road. As you walk along, you will see on your left **Lyndhurst Terrace**, which at one time in Hong Kong's history was a famous red-light district. A branch of the Hongkong and Shanghai Bank now stands on the corner of this once-notorious terrace. Continue along Hollywood Road. You will soon come to the grey stone walls of **Central Police Station** (5). Walk past the main entrance to the driveway which takes you into the open courtyard of the police compound. (Note: If you wish to take photographs, permission must be sought from the administrative office.)

In 1841 the Hong Kong Police started with a small force of 32 men who had been discharged as unfit for military service. As the colony's population increased, the higher incidence of crime made the creation of a more professional force a priority in the administration that was being established.

The task of organizing such a force was given to Captain William Caine of the 26th Cameronian Infantry Regiment. He was appointed Chief Magistrate on 30 April 1841. His first office was a matshed (a structure made of bamboo frames, palm leaf walls, and a thatched roof), which was immediately adjacent to the present Central Police Station.

The shortage and calibre of manpower made enforcement of the law very difficult. Captain Caine's methods of punishing lawbreakers were extremely harsh. He found that imprisonment was an unsuccessful deterrent to crime as some prisoners found life in prison preferable to living in cramped conditions at home. He therefore introduced public floggings and also imposed an 11 pm curfew on the Chinese populace. In 1843 an amendment to this rule required the Chinese not only to carry lanterns after 8 pm, but also to carry a pass if they were on the street after 10 pm. This curfew remained in force until 1897.

Charles May was appointed Captain Superintendent in 1845, and remained in the position for 17 years. During his tenure, May recruited Chinese and Indians into the force, and numerous police stations were opened throughout the colony.

In 1967, in recognition of their expert handling of the riots that broke out in Hong Kong as the Cultural Revolution was launched in China, the Police Force was bestowed with the prefix 'Royal' by Her Majesty Queen Elizabeth II. The Royal Hong Kong Police Force has continued to be efficient in dealing with all aspects of law and order.

As you stand at the top of the driveway, the red-brick building to your far left is the rear of the Magistracy, which was redeveloped in 1914. The Quarters Block, a three-storey building,

Jamia (Mohammedan) Mosque

had two storeys when it was built in 1864; the additional floor was added in 1905. Behind you is the Administrative Block, which opened in 1925. The Stores Block (warehouse) to the right is thought to have been the stables at one time and is now the home of the Accident Investigation Section of Traffic, Hong Kong Island.

The Magistracy and a jail were built in 1845. They were originally sited on the opposite side of Old Bailey Street where the Junior Police Officers' quarters now stand. Eventually, the jail proved to be inadequate and in the late 1850s the hulk of the naval vessel *Royal Saxon* was used as an auxiliary prison and was moored off Stonecutters Island which lies just west of Kowloon.

Various parts of the complex are known to have been interlinked with tunnels. A restored fire wagon, which now rests in the Officers' Mess, was recovered from one of these tunnels. The Mess also boasts the stuffed head of a wild tiger shot in Hong Kong in 1915, and the ship's bell of the former steamer *Norma*, which was launched in 1853.

On leaving Central Police Station, cross over by the traffic lights on your left to Pottinger Street. Continue down Pottinger Street and past Wellington Street until you reach Stanley Street. Turn right, and at 24 – 6 Stanley Street, you will see the **Luk Yu Teahouse** (6), one of the few remaining traditional teahouses in Hong Kong.

'Cha Kui' is the old local name for a Chinese teahouse. It used to cater exclusively for tea lovers. The sampling and enjoyment of tea has been a long-standing pastime with the people of Kwangtung Province, of which Hong Kong was once a part. A teahouse could be compared to an English pub where one goes regularly to meet friends in a convivial atmosphere. Teahouses also serve Chinese delicacies, and *dim sum*, which are bite-size snacks. *Dim sum*, literally translated, means 'To Touch the Heart'.

The Luk Yu Teahouse, named after a tea connoisseur of the Tang Dynasty (618 – 907), was built in the early 1930s. Originally it was in Wing Kut Street, but due to redevelopment in the area, it was relocated in 1975 to its present site in Stanley Street. The decor of the original building was faithfully reproduced, and the wooden façade and the calligraphic sign that originally hung outside were both taken to the new premises. Even the old equipment and furniture were used at the new site to maintain the ambience of a traditional teahouse. Some of the teas served at the Luk Yu Teahouse are extremely aromatic. This is because some of them are 'vintage' teas, having been stored by wholesalers for 20 years and by the teahouse for another five to ten years, before being offered for customer consumption. (Because this is a very popular teahouse, it is best to avoid the hours of noon to 1.30 pm.)

Having refreshed yourself with a cup of Chinese tea, continue down Stanley Street, turn left into D'Aguilar Street, then right into Queen's Road Central. Cross diagonally over Queen's Road on to the right-hand side of Pedder Street. It is difficult to believe that you are actually standing on what was once the waterfront of Victoria.

This walk ends here on Pedder Street. Between 3A Pedder Street and the Landmark Building, just above eye level, you will see a red oval **plaque** (7) which marks the waterfront of Hong Kong as it was in 1841.

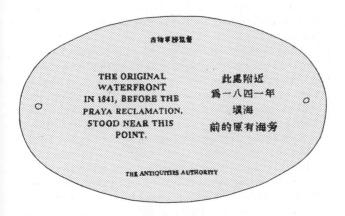

古物事務監督

THE ORIGINAL WATERFRONT IN 1841, BEFORE THE PRAYA RECLAMATION, STOOD NEAR THIS POINT.

此處附近 為一八四一年 填海 前的原有海旁

THE ANTIQUITIES AUTHORITY

Interesting Street Names on the Mid-Levels Walk

In the early days of Hong Kong, street names were by and large taken from British politicians, military men involved in the Opium Wars, and local civil servants. Hollywood Road, an exception, was named after the country house 'Hollywood Towers' owned by Sir John Davis, second Governor of Hong Kong. Caine, D'Aguilar, and Pedder were all members of the first Colonial Government appointed by Sir Henry Pottinger in 1843.

Caine Road was named after Captain William Caine, who was appointed Chief Magistrate in 1841. It seems appropriate that the road named for him is in the area of the Police Courts and Central Prison.

D'Aguilar Street was named after Major-General G.C. D'Aguilar, who served as Lieutenant-Governor under the first two governors of Hong Kong. As a result of his personal efforts in the early 1840s when tropical fever and dysentery caused many deaths, new barracks and hospitals were built. These new facilities helped to raise the standard of living in the colony and to lower the mortality rate of the troops.

Elgin Street was named after the Earl of Elgin. He was Governor-General of Canada in 1846. In 1857 he was sent as Plenipotentiary to China. In 1860 he and his troops stormed Peking and burned the Summer Palace. In October 1860 he brought about the signing of the Convention of Peking, from which Britain acquired Kowloon peninsula.

Lyndhurst Terrace was named after a former Lord Chancellor of England, Lord Lyndhurst. The terrace is called 'Bai Fa Gai' (Flower Show Street) by the local people.

Pedder Street was named after Lieutenant W. Pedder of the Royal Navy, who was appointed Harbour Master, having served as Marine Magistrate and Surveyor of Shipping during the period 1841 – 3.

Peel Street was named after Sir Robert Peel, Prime

Minister of Britain in 1834 and again in the early 1840s. Sir Robert's government levied a substantial tax on the colony's opium trade in 1846 in an effort to suppress it.

Pottinger Street was named after Sir Henry Pottinger, who served as the first Governor of Hong Kong from 20 May 1843 to 12 June 1844. Prior to that, he had served as Queen Victoria's Sole Plenipotentiary and Minister Extraordinary and in 1842 he negotiated the Treaty of Nanking by which Hong Kong became a British colony.

Rednaxela Terrace was probably named after Princess Alexandra in 1863. She later married King Edward VII.

Robinson Road commemorates Sir Hercules Robinson who was fifth Governor of Hong Kong from 9 September 1859 to 15 March 1865. The present Robinson Road was laid out in 1861. It was during Robinson's administration that the Kowloon peninsula was leased to Britain. The formal transfer of the Kowloon peninsula to the British was performed in a ceremony attended by a large group of local dignitaries and troops. A packet of soil was handed to Lord Elgin by a Cantonese mandarin as a symbolic token of cession.

Seymour Road was named after a Commander-in-Chief of the Naval Forces, Rear Admiral Sir Michael Seymour. Sir Michael fought the Chinese at Canton during the Arrow War of 1856. As a token of their gratitude and respect, the people of Hong Kong presented him with a plate valued at 2,000 guineas (£2,200) when he left in 1859.

Shelley Street was named after Adolphus E. Shelley, who was Clerk of Councils and Auditor General in 1844.

Stanley Street was named after Major-General Stanley, CB, who succeeded General D'Aguilar as General Officer in 1848.

Staunton Street was named after Sir George Staunton, translator of the original Chinese Statutes of the Tatsing Dynasty (penal code of China). In 1833 and again in 1836, Sir George advocated the establishment of a British outpost on the China coast for trade purposes.

St John's Cathedral

Victoria

Duration

Approximately 2 hours.

Description

On this walk you will see several late 19th-century Western-style homes, one of which today houses the Tea Ware Museum. Also from this period, you will walk by two original gas street lamps and an ice storage house. You will stroll through the Zoological and Botanical Gardens and visit the Roman Catholic and Anglican Cathedrals.

Points of Interest

Hong Kong Museum of Art (Open: 10 am – 6 pm daily except Thursdays. Sundays and some public holidays, open 1 pm – 6 pm), **Museum of Tea Ware** (Open: 10 am – 5 pm daily except Wednesdays and some public holidays), **Zoological and Botanical Gardens** (Open: 6 am – 10 pm daily; no dogs allowed), **Catholic Cathedral, Bishop's House, French Mission Building** (Open: daily during business hours), **Anglican Cathedral.**

Starting Point

'Star' Ferry Pier, Central, Hong Kong Island (中環天星碼頭).

How to Get There

From Kowloon　　Take the Star Ferry or the MTR (underground railway) to Central, Hong Kong Island and then follow the directions below.

From Hong Kong Island　　Walk through the pedestrian underpass beside the Mandarin Hotel to the 'Star' Ferry Pier, or take a taxi to the 'Star' Ferry Pier, Hong Kong Island.

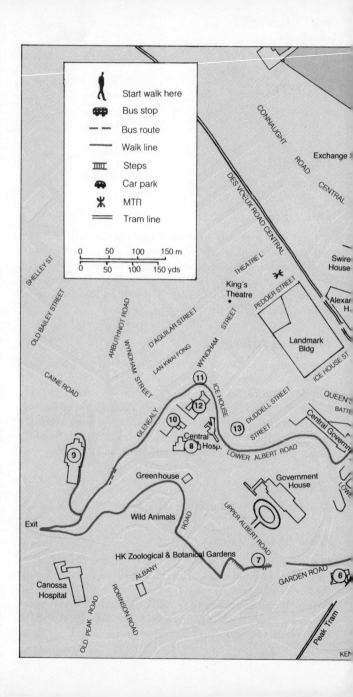

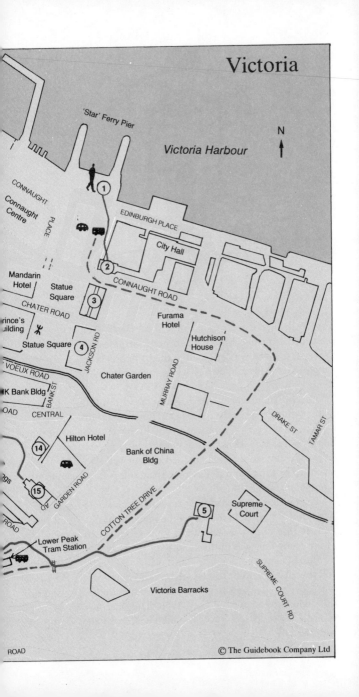

Victoria

Victoria Harbour

'Star' Ferry Pier

N

CONNAUGHT PLACE

Connaught Centre

EDINBURGH PLACE

City Hall

CONNAUGHT ROAD

Mandarin Hotel

Statue Square

CHATER ROAD

Prince's Building

Statue Square

JACKSON RD

Furama Hotel

Hutchison House

Chater Garden

MURRAY ROAD

VOEUX ROAD

NK Bank Bldg

BANK ST

OAD

CENTRAL

Hilton Hotel

Bank of China Bldg

DRAKE ST

TAMAR ST

ngs

GARDEN ROAD

COTTON TREE DRIVE

Supreme Court

ROAD

Lower Peak Tram Station

Victoria Barracks

SUPREME COURT RD

ROAD

© The Guidebook Company Ltd

Gas street lamp

This walk begins in front of the **'Star' Ferry Pier** (1) on land reclaimed from the harbour and now forming part of **Central District**. Central was originally called Victoria after Queen Victoria of Great Britain, during whose reign Hong Kong became a British colony.

As you stand facing the harbour, read the following short history of the Star Ferry before going on to the Museum of Art.

'The Star Ferry Company as we know it today came into being on 1st May 1898 having bought out a previous passenger ferry operator. The fleet consisted of four vessels whose names all ended in "Star" and it is assumed that this is the reason for the Company's name.

The new company had very close ties with the Hong Kong & Kowloon Wharf & Godown Company and the Kowloon Ferry Pier at this time was actually within Godown property. The Hong Kong Pier was in the vicinity of Ice House Street.

Shortly after commencing business, new ferries were built and these later became double-enders and two deckers. As Kowloon developed, a new fleet was again built in the 1920's, and this fleet remained in service until 1956. The fleet now consists of ten (diesel) vessels.' (Quoted from The 'Star' Ferry Company, Limited.)

The main service is between Hong Kong Island and Tsim Sha Tsui, and today over 100,000 passengers are ferried daily between the hours of 6 am and 11.30 pm. The ride across Victoria Harbour provides spectacular water and city views and is probably the best bargain in town!

Now, with your back to the harbour, the Star Ferry carpark is in front of you and the City Hall is to its left. Walk between the two buildings, enter the High Block of the City Hall, and take the elevator to the 10/11th floors, to the **Hong Kong Museum of Art** (2). This museum is well worth a visit as it holds a vast collection of Oriental art.

Upon leaving the High Block, look for a bright green sign marked 'Peak Tram' (between the City Hall building and the carpark). From here, take the free double-decker bus directly to the Lower Peak Tram Station. The bus leaves daily every 20 minutes between 9 am and 6.50 pm. On a fine day, it is particularly nice to sit on the top deck for this five-minute trip. (On weekends the bus may be very crowded, so you may want to walk to the **Lower Peak Tram Station** at St John's Building on Garden Road up the hill past the Hilton Hotel.)

As the bus pulls out on to Connaught Road, straight in front of you is a tall **Monument** dedicated to the **Glorious Dead,** 1914 – 18 and 1939 – 45 (3). Behind the monument is the **Legislative Council Building** (4). The Legislative Council Building, formerly the Supreme Court Building, was designed by leading British architects Ashton Webb and Ingress Bell. It was constructed during the period 1899 – 1910 to house the Courts of Justice in Victoria and was formally opened in 1912 by Governor Sir Frederick Lugard, the 14th Governor of Hong Kong. Above the main portico, overlooking Statue Square, is the blindfolded statue of Justice, the Greek Goddess Themis. This lovely granite building was converted to the Legislative Council Building in 1984 – 5 when the judiciary moved to the new Supreme Court Building, Queensway. In 1984 the building was declared an historic landmark.

Connaught Road is said to be named after the son of Queen Victoria, the Duke of Connaught, known as Prince Arthur of Connaught. Prince Arthur visited Hong Kong in 1900 when he laid the foundation stone for the new praya (waterfront road) reclamation scheme. In 1841 the shoreline was about a block north of Queen's Road. By 1889 the land had been extended north to the harbour by approximately another city block, still leaving what is now the site of Alexandra House, Prince's Building, Statue Square, the Legislative Council Building, and the Furama Hotel in the sea.

At the Lower Peak Tram Station where the bus lets you out, you will see the sign, '**Cotton Tree Drive**'. Cotton Tree is the common name of the 'Bombax Malabaricum' which flowers around April and produces large hollow pods filled with a cotton-like fibre. The fibre provides stuffing for cushions and the dried flowers are used medicinally. It is said that only when the tree is in full bloom can winter clothes be put away. However, some Chinese feel it is not safe to store cold-weather clothes until after the Dragon Boat Festival in June!

Follow this sign via the Pedestrian Subway under Cotton Tree Drive. As you emerge, walk down the hill a short distance towards the harbour. Take the first road to the right and immediately turn left into the driveway marked '**Flagstaff House, Museum of Tea Ware**' (5). A pleasant walk up this drive brings you to the museum. On the hill are some 100-year-old buildings which were the living quarters of the officers serving in Victoria Barracks. Most recently, they have been government quarters for Hong Kong civil servants. This area is now scheduled for redevelopment as parkland.

Flagstaff House was built in 1844 – 6 and is one of the oldest Western-style buildings still standing in Hong Kong. Until 1978 it was the residence and office of the Commander of the British Forces in Hong Kong. Today, its high ceilings and deep verandas vividly recall the days before air-conditioning. Its beautiful wooden floors and fine fireplaces are also reminiscent of an earlier era. In 1981 the Urban Council took over the management of the building and restored it, as near as possible, to its original 19th-century appearance. It was opened as the Museum of Tea Ware and now houses the magnificent K.S. Lo Collection of Tea Ware and related objects.

According to the museum brochure, the Chinese drank tea over 2,000 years ago and were the first people to cultivate tea plants. But it was not until the ninth century that tea drinking spread from China to other countries. In fact, the Japanese tea ceremonies follow the Chinese tradition of the Song Dynasty

(960 – 1279). It was not until the 17th century that tea drinking spread to Europe. The grounds of the museum are lovely, and the colourful gardens attract many bridal parties from the Marriage Registry across the road for wedding photographs.

After visiting the museum and grounds, retrace your steps along Cotton Tree Drive to the Lower Peak Tram Station.

Cross Garden Road at the traffic lights, turn left and follow the blue and white signs marked 'Zoological and Botanical Gardens'. Walk up the hill about 90 metres (98 yards) and look to your left at the large white colonial building, **The Helena May** (6), a private residential club. The Helena May was formally opened in 1916 by Hong Kong's 15th Governor, Sir Henry May. The Helena May provided accommodation for working women passing through or residing in Hong Kong. Under the guidance of Lady May and the generosity of Sir E. Kadoorie and several prominent local residents, plans were drawn up for an 'adapted Renaissance style' building comprising an office, reading room, dining room, lounge, two classrooms, and a small library. The upper storey was to accommodate eight bedrooms, with provision for four more if needed. Many early records were lost during the Second World War, but it is known that the Japanese occupied the building and immediately after the war it was the headquarters for the Royal Air Force. In 1947 The Helena May was re-established for its original purpose.

Today there are about 41 residents, 1,096 members, and an extensive library of over 16,000 books. Talks, short courses, and musical evenings are held on a regular basis for members. Certainly, The Helena May is an oasis in time.

Continue walking up Garden Road, and take the steps to the small road that runs along the white wall surrounding **Government House**, the home of Hong Kong's Governor. The main entrance of Government House is on **Upper Albert Road**, a road built by over 2,000 convicts, according to Surveyor General Cleverly. Later, you will have a better view of Government House from the Botanical Gardens.

Early administrators of the colony soon realized the need for a Government House. Planning was started by the Surveyor General, Mr Cleverly, in 1845 and the site was prepared in 1848. However, actual construction work did not begin until October 1851. It was finally completed and occupied in 1855 by Sir John

Bowring, the fourth Governor. To celebrate the jubilee of Government House, an annex was added in 1891. During the Japanese occupation of Hong Kong, the main building was largely rebuilt and the tower added by 26-year-old Japanese engineer Seichi Fujimura.

Turn left, cross the road, and walk through the underpass of Upper Albert Road until you see a sign marked 'Hong Kong Zoological and Botanical Gardens'. Turn right and go up the stairs. At the top of these stairs, you will see on your left the large concrete steps under the overpass. Go up these steps, and at the fork, take the wide steps to the right. You are now at the large entry gates of the **Hong Kong Zoological and Botanical Gardens** (7).

One of the first efforts to create a public Botanical Garden was in 1848 when a proposal was made at a meeting of the Royal Asiatic Society in Hong Kong. The government was approached, but Sir George Bonham vetoed the proposal because of the lack of funds. Sir John Bowring, who succeeded Sir George, was very interested in establishing a public garden and stressed both scientific and economic reasons for such a project. In about 1860 the Surveyor General's Department laid out a garden south of Government House. In 1861 Thomas Donaldson was appointed Curator, and seeds and plants were ordered from Australia and Europe. The gardens were opened to the public in 1864. In 1871 Charles Ford became Curator and continued to introduce plants from Australia and China. It is said that in 1882, about one-tenth of Hong Kong was planted with approximately 25 million trees and that its appearance was very much improved. In 1975 the name changed to Zoological and Botanical Gardens. Today, approximately three million people visit the gardens each year.

As you enter, you pass under a **Stone Archway** engraved: 'In Memory of the Chinese Who Died Loyal to the Allied Cause in the Wars of 1914 – 18 and 1939 – 45'. After this monument, take the steps to the right marked 'Office'. At the top, with the fountain in front of you, walk left towards the waterfall and aviary. At this point you may wish to explore further the aviary and the gardens surrounding the fountain.

Afterwards, return to the waterfall, and with it in front of you, turn right and continue along the path until you see signs for 'Children's Playground' and 'Aviary' pointing left and

'Refreshment Kiosk' and 'Office' pointing right. Go straight through the underpass which leads to the wild animal exhibits and the greenhouse.

At the top of the underpass, turn right and follow the sign marked 'Exit' and 'Greenhouse'. About 13 metres (15 yards) past the greenhouse, below and to the right across the street, stands a two-storeyed Victorian building which was originally built as an Anglican **Church Guesthouse** (8).

Many missionaries and their families travelled in and out of China and this house provided them with welcome shelter. It remained a guesthouse until after the Second World War. One of its better known residents was Han Suyin, who wrote the book *A Many Splendoured Thing*. She lived here while in Medical School at Hong Kong University.

Bishop's House

Walk on, then climb the first steps to the left and continue to bear right as you pass the Bornean orang-utangs. Continue along this most pleasant path to the right for approximately 120 metres (130 yards), at which point you can see the **Roman Catholic Cathedral** (9) peeking through two buildings. Continue through the turnstiles at the exit gate and take a hard right turn down the steep hill to the small roundabout. The driveway will lead you up to the cathedral where you can walk around and go inside if you wish.

The Roman Catholic Cathedral was completed in 1888. Many of the pillars supporting the roof were donated by members of the community, particularly the Portuguese Roman Catholics from Macau who had come to live in Hong Kong. The west windows are over 80 years old and were made in Toulouse, France, by the renowned stained glass artist, Gesta. On either side of the north entrance are two altars built from the altar of the first Roman Catholic Cathedral in Hong Kong, which burned twice at its site on Wellington Street. A memorial tablet to the first representative of the Pope in Hong Kong is set in the floor at the north entrance.

Go back down the drive and take the road to the left. At the first intersection, Upper Albert and Glenealy Roads, follow the pedestrian subway on your right to Glenealy.

Glenealy was originally a ravine called 'Elliot's Vale' after Captain Charles Elliot who was the colony's first administrator in 1841. This area was once described as 'the most romantic glen of the island'. Continue down the hill for about two blocks. On your right is **St Paul's Episcopal Church** (10). The present structure was built in 1911.

In 1843 the government provided land for the Anglican colonial Chaplain, Vincent Stanton, to build a school for Chinese who wished to study English in preparation for the Anglican ministry. The school started classes in the newly constructed Bishop's House, which you will see later.

The first Bishop of Hong Kong, the Reverend George Smith, arrived in 1850. The Bishop's House became St Paul's School in 1851 and it also provided a chapel for Chinese Anglican worship. Later, the government provided a grant to St Paul's to train interpreters for the consular services. Unfortunately, none of the graduates took up the ministry or became interpreters, but rather used this valuable English-language training in the private sector.

In 1863 St Paul's established a college in Bonham Road across from the University of Hong Kong. The present St Paul's Episcopal Church, here on Glenealy, was opened for Chinese Anglican worship in 1911. Sunday services are still held in Cantonese.

At the traffic light, stop and look at the narrow brick and stucco building across from you, between Wyndham Street (reportedly once known as 'the Fleet Street of Hongkong') and Lower Albert Road. It has the date 1913 engraved in stone at roof level. This was the **Dairy Farm Building** (11), the company's former town depot, with one of the first ice houses of the colony.

Walk along the right side of this building on Lower Albert Road. Today, the building is occupied by the Fringe Club and the Foreign Correspondents Club (FCC). Stand in front of the FCC and look up to the right at the **Bishop's House** (12). Cross over to the upper road, Lower Albert Road, which goes uphill. Continue along this road until you reach Central Hospital on your right. At the steps on your left, stop for a moment and look down at two of the original **gas street lamps** (13) on Ice House Street.

Ice House Street was so named because of one of its early tenants. An article in the *Hong Kong Telegraph* of 13 June 1883 stated: 'It appears that many years ago, the Hong Kong Government granted the temporary use of a piece of ground in what is now known as Ice House Lane to the Ice Association of Hong Kong for the purpose of erecting a store-room for ice and on the express condition that the Association would always keep on the premises a supply of ice for hospital purposes.... In those days, the ice was not manufactured in the Colony but came by sailing vessels from America and subsequently it had to be stored in immense quantities.'

A few hundred metres along Lower Albert Road are the Central Government Buildings. Turn left through the entrance, and walk through the carpark and down the hill to Battery Path towards the brick building with dark green shutters. This is the **French Mission Building** (14), which houses the Government Information Services Department. Until recently, it was used as the Victoria District Court.

Early records show that a house was built in the early 1840s on this site for the Acting Superintendent of Trade. After several ownership changes, it was bought by the Missions Etrangères in 1915. In 1953 the site and building were bought back by the government.

The wide staircase, solid window sills, and ornamentation about the lintels are suggestive of the early 1900s. The room under the cupola was used as a chapel. You can still see the mosaic floor and Gothic-style east windows. Inspection of this building is allowed on weekdays during business hours. On the right side of the building is a plaque with additional historical information.

Beside the French Mission Building is **St John's Cathedral** (15), the Anglican (Episcopal) Church, one of the earliest Christian churches in Hong Kong and maybe the first Anglican Cathedral in East Asia.

The foundation stone was laid in 1847 by the second Governor, Sir John Davis, and his Coat of Arms was set in the north face of the bell tower. The first service was held in 1849. After enlarging the nave (the main part of the church interior) in 1865, the cathedral was completed to its present size. During the Second World War, the Japanese army used the cathedral for its headquarters, and in the course of their occupation, much of it was damaged. However, the main doors made from the wood of HMS *Tamar*, a stores depot ship docked in Victoria Harbour from 1897 to 1941, are original, as is the pulpit, although the canopy is of a later date. The stone font (a receptacle for baptismal water), though damaged, stands in the north transept. The marble screen behind the high altar is the work of the Victorian church architect William Butterfield.

After the war, private citizens and companies contributed time and money to the restoration of the cathedral, which has continued to be the centre of the Anglican community of Hong Kong and Macau. All the stained glass windows were donated, including the south window which was given by the former worshippers of the Holy Trinity Cathedral, Shanghai. The wooden screen at the end of the choir stall was designed by a long-time English resident architect, Eric Faber, and was constructed without nails. On the south side of the aisle in St Michael's Chapel is a reredos (screen) made by an English soldier imprisoned in Shamshuipo in Kowloon during the war. On the other side of the aisle is the Quiet Chapel, a place for individual worship and contemplation.

As you leave the cathedral, notice the hanging boards with the names of past clergy. The colourful mosaic on the entry floor is of an octagonal design incorporating the symbols of the Trinity. At the top of the eagle is the symbol of St John the Evangelist and, in the centre, a Nestorian Cross replica. In the cathedral grounds is the **Memorial Cross**, dedicated to those who fell in the First World War. Near it is the **gravestone** of a Private Maxwell, who died near this area during the Battle of Hong Kong. The cathedral, which is the last stop on this walk, is open daily for private devotion.

There are several ways to return to Central. One is to walk along either side of the cathedral to Garden Road and follow the road down the hill to the Hilton Hotel on Queen's Road Central. Another way is to return to the entrance of the French Mission Building and walk downhill on Battery Path which leads to Queen's Road Central and Ice House Street across from the Landmark Building.

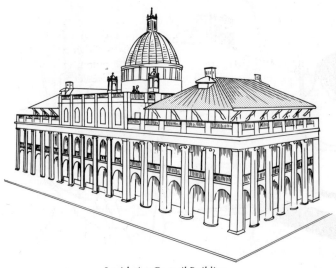

Legislative Council Building

Amah Rock

Wanchai Gap

Duration

Approximately 3 hours.

Description

You will travel by Peak Tram, double-decker bus and foot to some unusual and lovely areas of Hong Kong, including Victoria Peak, a pedestrian stretch of Bowen Road, a lovely 30–40 minute walk, which will lead you finally into Wanchai. You will experience unforgettable views, stroll along peaceful paths, and visit fascinating temples.

Points of Interest

Peak Tram, Bowen Road Lover's Shrine, Pak Tai Temple, Old Post Office, Hung Sing Temple.

Starting Point

Lower Peak Tram Station, St John's Building, 33 Garden Road, Central（山頂纜車總站）.

How to Get There

From Kowloon　Take the Star Ferry or the MTR (underground railway) to Central, Hong Kong Island and then follow the directions below.

From Hong Kong Island　Walk up the hill from the Hilton Hotel on the corner of Queen's Road Central and Garden Road, or take a taxi to the Lower Peak Tram Station.

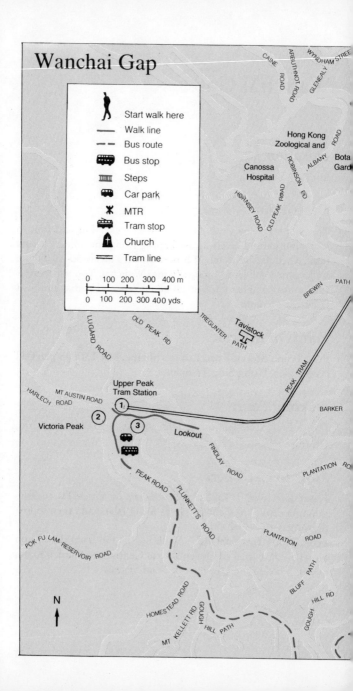

Wanchai Gap

Start walk here
Walk line
Bus route
Bus stop
Steps
Car park
MTR
Tram stop
Church
Tram line

0   100 200 300 400 m
0   100 200 300 400 yds.

CAINE ROAD
ARBUTHNOT ROAD
WYNDHAM STREET
GLENEALY ROAD

Hong Kong Zoological and

Canossa Hospital

ROBINSON RD
ALBANY ROAD
Bota Gard

HORNSEY ROAD
OLD PEAK ROAD

BREWIN PATH

LUGARD ROAD
OLD PEAK RD
TREGUNTER PATH
Tavistock PATH

PEAK TRAM

Upper Peak Tram Station

HARLECH ROAD
MT AUSTIN ROAD

BARKER

Victoria Peak

Lookout

FINDLAY ROAD

PLANTATION RO

PEAK ROAD
PLUNKETT'S ROAD

POK FU LAM RESERVOIR ROAD

PLANTATION ROAD

BLUFF PATH

HOMESTEAD ROAD
MT KELLETT ROAD
GOUGH HILL PATH
GOUGH HILL RD

N

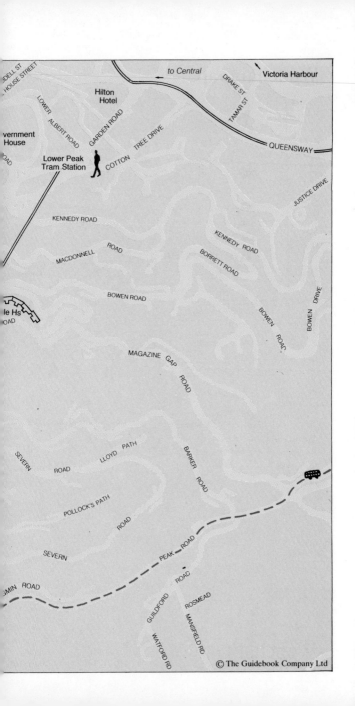

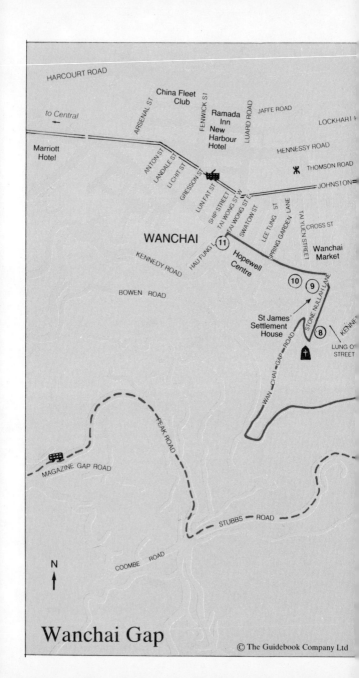

Wanchai Gap

© The Guidebook Company Ltd

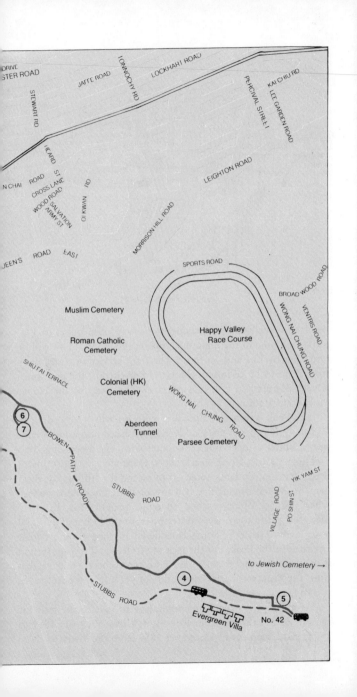

The old Peak Hotel

Begin this 'walk' by purchasing a one-way tram ticket to Victoria Peak, one of the highest points on the island. (You will be returning by bus and on foot.) The tram service operates daily from 7 am to 12 midnight. (Note: On weekends, the peak tram is very popular, so you may want to take a taxi to the Upper Peak Tram Station.)

The **Peak Tram** is a funicular railway, which according to *Webster's Dictionary* is 'a cable railway ascending a mountain; one in which an ascending car counterbalances a descending car'.

During Hong Kong's early days, there were very few places where foreign residents could go to escape the stifling hot summers of the settlements that had spread along the waterfront and where disease often reached epidemic proportions. By 1847 many people in town were suffering from the heat and dying of fever and dysentery. Some considered moving to the cooler environs of the Peak, but the lack of services and transportation discouraged them. Also, it must be remembered that at that time, the Peak was barren rock and not yet lush and beautiful as it is today.

To inspire the expatriate community to take to the hills for reasons of health, Hercules Robinson, Governor from 1859 to 1865, had a path cut in December 1859 from the lower levels to

Victoria Peak. He also began to plant the area with eucalyptus trees and shrubs imported from Australia. Along this path, a residential district started to develop. Many of the *hongs* started to build summer houses on the Peak for their senior employees, and by 1876 it had become a popular resort. ('Hong' is a Chinese name for commercial firms which trade with foreign countries. Many of these original trading houses, such as Jardine, Swire, Wharf, and Hutchison, still do business in Hong Kong today.)

At that time, the only means of transport to and from the upper levels was by sedan chair. The trip cost 15 cents per half hour and 25 cents an hour for the upper levels, and 75 cents an hour for the hill districts, which required four bearers.

By 1883 people were tired of the time and effort required to get to the Peak by this means of transportation. Seeking an alternative, several businessmen applied for permission to build a tramway from St John's Place to Victoria Gap on the Peak. After obtaining the rights, they sold them in 1885 to Phineas Kyrie and A. Findlay Smith. It was actually Smith who started construction of the tramway because he wanted to build a hotel (Peak Hotel) next to the Upper Peak Tram Station.

On 30 May 1888 the tram was opened by Governor Sir William Des Voeux and, for 60 cents, the wealthy residents of Hong Kong could escape the oppressive summer heat of the city. The tram prompted many more residents to build summer — and ultimately permanent — houses in the cool hills. The Peak Tram was the only means of regular transport to the Peak until the first road was built in 1924.

The original Lower Peak Tram Terminal was constructed of wood. Between 1888 and 1972, both lower and upper terminals were rebuilt twice. In 1926 a new terminal was built to accommodate the larger tramcars that were necessary due to the increase in the number of passengers. This terminal remained in use until 1972, when it was modified to conform with the Peak Tower Complex constructed between 1969 and 1972. The Lower Terminal at St John's Building was rebuilt for a third time in 1983. Originally, the cars were made of wood, but today's aluminium cars, built in 1959, are larger but lighter. In keeping with progress, once again plans are underway for further modernization of the terminal and tram cars.

Initially, the haulage plant was steam powered, but it changed to electric traction in 1926. The 1,370-metre (4,500-foot) long path of the tram is almost the same as in 1888, running from 24 metres (80 feet) above sea level at the lower terminal to 398 metres (1,305 feet) above sea level at Victoria Gap. The seven-minute ride provides breathtaking views of the harbour and countryside. Many Hong Kong residents commute by the tram daily. In order to board the tram, they simply flag it down at the stops, and to get off, they press the appropriate button under the windows: Kennedy, Macdon'l (Macdonnell), May and Barker Roads. May Road has the steepest section of track, with a gradient of 27 degrees to the horizontal.

When you leave the tramcar, walk through the **Peak Tower** (1). On this main level is a balcony lookout with telescopes. The other floors contain a variety of shops — souvenir shops, a grocery store, a bank, and restaurants. It is worth taking the elevator to the top for a panoramic view ($1.00).

As you exit on the other side of the tower, you will see across from you the **Peak Café** (2), which, according to a local newspaper, is a converted rickshaw shack that has also been marked for redevelopment. To its right are three roads: Harlech, Mt Austin, and Lugard. Go over to the entrance to Harlech Road and look at the map showing the 'Scenic Walks and Jogging-Fitness Trails' which circle the Peak. There is a one-hour walk with magnificent views, almost 360 degrees, of Hong Kong Island, which is especially magical at sunrise or sunset. (Note: This walk is not included in the approximate duration of three hours.) This area provides an ideal vantage point and once even served as a lookout and fortified headquarters of a Chinese pirate, Cheung Po Tsai, who between 1806 and 1810 became infamous for his daring exploits. He later moved to neighbouring Cheung Chau Island, 11 kilometres (seven miles) southwest of Hong Kong Island.

Across from the map, notice the 'P' (parking) Rickshaws sign. Rickshaws were once a popular means of travel in old Hong Kong, but now they are used only for charity races here on the Peak or for photography sessions at the Star Ferry.

Go back across the road into Findlay Road, keeping the carpark/bus terminal on your right. Look up to the right at the stone foundations of what was once the **Peak Hotel** (3). Mr Findlay Smith opened a splendid hotel in 1900 and called it the

Peak Hotel. It was a popular gathering place for social events. The building was destroyed by fire in 1938. Continue on Findlay Road past this site to a fabulous lookout.

Return to the parking lot and look for a No. 15 'Central Terminal' sign. A double-decker bus runs about every 15 minutes and the 10 – 15-minute ride is quite breathtaking, especially in the upper deck at the front.

On the right, exquisite views of the Pokfulam Reservoir Aberdeen town, Aberdeen Reservoirs, Deepwater Bay, and the South China Sea unfold. The winding route loops into Guildford Road for the bus to pick up passengers, then returns to Peak Road. At the first intersection, the Victoria Harbour side of Hong Kong can be seen on the left. The bus follows a spectacular panoramic route along Peak Road into **Stubbs Road**.

Stubbs Road opened in 1924. Prior to that time, the only means of 'wheeled transport' to the Peak was the tramway. The road was named after Sir Reginald Stubbs who was Governor from 1919 to 1925.

As you twist and turn down Stubbs Road, you will see on the left an **old Chinese house** (4) with a green tiled roof. This house was built in the early 1920s by a wealthy Chinese businessman.

Pay particular attention here — if you are on the top deck of the bus, go downstairs because you will get off at the second stop after the old house (across from Highcliff Apartments, No. 42 Stubbs Road).

Walk back 40 – 50 metres (50 – 60 yards) on the same side of the road to the steps located directly opposite the entrance to No. 42 Stubbs Road; these lead down to **Bowen Path (Road)**. This road was originally a very narrow footpath running beside a five-kilometre (three-mile) aqueduct from Tai Tam Reservoir to Central District. From the top of the stairs, you will probably smell the incense before you can locate the red corrugated roof that houses the shrine dedicated to the Earth God of Bowen Road. Walk down the two flights of steps until you come to the stairs with the red railing along the side of the hill. Walk up these for a closer look at the **Earth God Shrine** (5).

Earth Gods (T'u Ti) have been worshipped in China for thousands of years. Their earliest beginnings were connected with animism of the Neolithic Age. They protect small communities and rule over the intimate affairs of the neighbourhood.

T'u Ti listen to rumours; log births, deaths, and marriages; and comfort the sick and downtrodden. Usually found outside, most of the shrines are small with a rough stone image and a trough for incense or simply a blackened niche in a wall.

Return to the main steps and turn left at the bottom on to Bowen Road. A walk along this lovely, lush path that is quiet and serene during the week, but crowded with joggers, lovers, and dog walkers on the weekends, will take 30–40 minutes. A numbered fitness course (Parcours) decreases in number as you continue walking. Just past Parcours No. 17, you can look out over **Happy Valley**, the **Racecourse**, and the **Cemetery**.

In the early days of the territory, Western District was one of the first suburbs to be occupied. That area is said to have had frequent malaria epidemics, and it soon lost its appeal. The settlers began looking to Eastern District here in Wong Nai Chung Valley, now Happy Valley, in the mistaken belief that being relatively distant from the sea it was therefore a healthier area. Soon, elegant terraced houses were built and Wong Nai Chung Valley became the residential area in which to live. Its name in Chinese means 'Yellow Mud Stream' and the valley, living up to its name, unfortunately turned out to be a swamp. After heavy rainfall, it was infested with mosquitoes and many people died of fever. In the interests of health and sanitation, the area was drained on 23 April 1845, and the cultivation of rice on the island was forbidden.

An Earth God shrine

The racetrack now stands on what was the flattest piece of land on the island. It was previously used as a military camp, but soon after the land was drained, both residents and the military moved to healthier areas. It is said that horse-racing was started by the military, but dates vary from 1841 to 1846. According to an article in the December 1846 *China Mail Newspaper,* Hong Kong's first newspaper, '...two races were to be held that month, but initially there was only one race meeting a year, usually at Chinese New Year.'

The Royal Hong Kong Jockey Club was founded in 1884 to improve racing. In 1971 the club switched from amateur to professional jockeys. The Jockey Club makes a significant contribution to the community in its support of schools, clinics, parks, and cultural centres. The racing season runs from October to May. Approximately US$40 million is bet per race day. When compared to US$5 million per race day in the United States, you can see how important racing is in Hong Kong!

In the same valley, opposite the racecourse, is a unique cemetery. It is actually five separate cemeteries: Muslim, Catholic, Colonial, Parsee, and Jewish. If you approach it from Queen's Road East, the first is the **Muslim Cemetery**, and next to that is the **Catholic Cemetery**, established in 1847. The largest cemetery is the **Colonial (Hong Kong) Cemetery**, dating from 1845. Of historical interest are many old headstones of missionaries, civil servants, and naval and military personnel. One of Britain's most famous naval officers, Lord Napier, the first Chief Superintendent of the opening of trade in China, is buried here. Beyond the Colonial burial ground are the **Parsee Cemetery**, built in 1852, and the **Jewish Cemetery**, sanctified in 1855.

Further along Bowen Road, just after Parcours No. 14, you will come upon the **Bowen Road Lover's Stone Garden** (6), a fascinating place with shrines, incense, and coloured foil windmills. Go into the Stone Garden and you will see the steps up to the **Yan Yuen Sek** (7), the 'Rock of Predestined Lot in Marriage'. These steep zigzag stairs lead to the nine-metre (30-foot) monolith and a wonderful view of Wanchai and Victoria Harbour.

The Yan Yuen Sek shrine is known locally as 'Amah Rock'. It is not known when the rock was first used as a shrine, but it was probably around the end of the 19th century. Devotees are mostly unmarried girls, wives, and widows, who burn joss sticks and pray for ideal husbands and sons. Offerings of roasted pig, fruit, and wine are placed near the shrine and handmade stickers with special written requests are stuck on the stone.

The best time to visit the shrine is during the Maiden's Festival on the seventh day of the seventh month of the Chinese lunar calendar, when the legend of the Cowherd and the Weaving Girl is commemorated.

Myth has it that while the seven daughters of the Kitchen God were bathing in the river, a passing cowherd stole the clothes belonging to the prettiest sister. When she came out of the water and discovered her loss, she went to the cowherd and demanded her clothes. Once the cowherd saw the young girl naked, he was obliged to marry her. So they married and lived happily for three years. Then the gods ordered her back to heaven to continue her job of weaving clothes. They decreed that the lovers should be allowed a glimpse of each other only once a year. When the cowherd died, he was turned into an Immortal with the aid of his magic cow. His hopes of being reunited with his wife were frustrated, however, by the Queen of Heaven, who was furious at the thought of losing her seamstress again. She swept her magic hairpin across the sky, creating the Milky Way, with the weaving girl on one side and the cowherd on the other. Although they are within sight of each other, they are unable to get together except once a year on the double seventh. On this day, flocks of magpies form a bridge so that the lovers can once again meet.

Continue along Bowen Road, enjoying the numerous shrines along the way, until you reach the junction. Take the sharp right turn down **Wan Chai Gap Road,** which is said to be the oldest path to the south side of the island. As you approach the end of the road, you will see the St James' Settlement Building in red and yellow with white silhouetted figures.

Turn right into Kennedy Road and walk to St James' Church. Cross the road at the pedestrian crossing and walk down the steps to **Stone Nullah Lane** ('nullah' means 'gully or ravine'). Turn right into Lung On Street to see the **Pak Tai Temple** (8), built in 1863.

In the Main Hall (Temple of the Jade Emperor) stands a 3.3-

metre (ten-foot) copper statue of Pak Tai cast in 1604 during the Ming Dynasty. Pak Tai, Emperor of the North, was reputed to be a prince who lived in the Chou Dynasty (1122 – 770 BC). Pak Tai is the Military Protector and the 'First General of Heaven's Armies'. His title, Hsuan T'ien Shang Ti, means 'Dark Heaven Superior Ruler', and when chaos reigns on earth, he is believed to descend from heaven to restore harmony.

Behind this large statue are four life-size figures guarding Pak Tai on the central altar. They are General Nga Cha, Warrior, Man Cheong, Scholar, Wah Kwong, Warrior, and Yuen Tan, who is reputed to ride a tiger to frighten off evil spirits.

On the temple's left wall are the 60-year-cycle figures, the Tai Sui or gods of the year. Prayers are made to the god whose number is the same age as the person praying. Once you reach 60 years of age, you start all over again. It is interesting to note that the Chinese consider a child to be one year old at birth, so the parents of a newborn child would pray to the 'number one god'.

At the time of writing, there are six smaller shrines, three on each side of the middle Pak Tai shrine. From left to right as you stand facing the main altar, they are: Kwang Kung (God of War), Pao Kung (God of Justice), and Taoist Immortal Lau T'ai-ho (Patron of Florists). To the other side of the main altar are Three Buddhas (The Three Pure Ones), Kuan Yin (Goddess of Mercy), and Yuan Kung (keeper of harmony in the home).

As you come out of the Main Hall, Dragon Mother Hall is to your left. Lung Mo (Mother of Dragon) was born in Yui Sing village in Kwangtung Province. Because of her merciful qualities — she listens to each and every request — she was deified on her death. Inside there is a workshop where master craftsmen practise what is slowly becoming a lost art — creating burial offerings from bamboo and coloured paper. The Chinese believe in a life after death, and they prepare for the next world by sending paper copies of worldly goods to the deceased and to their ancestors. Clothing, furniture, cars, airplanes, money, and other articles of necessity and luxury are made and burned. The smoke carries the essence of these paper images to the 'ghost of the deceased' so that he will be comfortable in his next life.

If you walk through the workshop you will come to an inner courtyard with yet another building, The Palace of the Fortune

God. On the other side of the Main Hall is the Three Precious Palace Funeral Service and Ancestral Tablets Hall.

Further down at the end of the courtyard, the Tai Zau Stove Shrine protects against malicious slander. To ask for such protection, take a piece of paper, one with incense holes burned in it, and beat it on the ground while praying. Then throw the paper into the incinerator to send it up to Tai Zau.

Just as you are leaving the temple courtyard, turn around and look up at the statues on the roof, which are Shih-wan ware. This pottery was made in kilns which date back to the Ming period, when it was known as five-colour pottery. This handmade pottery is still being produced today in the area of Shih-wan in Kwangtung Province in China.

Go down the stairs and across Lung On Street and continue down Stone Nullah Lane, passing the front of St James' Settlement House. At the first major intersection, notice the Wanchai fresh food market across from you before turning left into Queen's Road East which, like the rest of Queen's Road, runs parallel to the original waterfront. Continue walking until you see 237 Queen's Road East, the Cheong On Pawn Shop (9).

It is believed that until the early 1940s, families stored their bulky clothing in the local pawn shop because of lack of space in their own homes. Today, mainly jewellery is pawned, but if it is not redeemed within four months it can be sold.

In Hong Kong, the interiors of all pawn shops look alike. From the street there are no visible main doors, but a solid wooden screen gives privacy to any transactions conducted. The counter inside is high and rather intimidating for the client who has to look up at the clerk peering down from behind a security grille.

After crossing Wan Chai Gap Road, take a look at **Wan Chai Post Office** (10), Hong Kong's oldest post office. According to an article in an old Chinese newspaper kept at the Post Office, the site on which it stands was part of the waterfront in 1841.

The next street you cross is **Spring Garden Lane**, which was once a fashionable residential area — an elegant praya along the seafront.

Hong Kong's third Governor, Sir Samuel George Bonham (1848 – 54) and his family lived in Spring Gardens before Government House was built. Their first house, which today would be in the centre of Wanchai, is said to have belonged to the firm of Blenkin Rawson. At the time, it was about a mile out of town and surrounded by half an acre of beautiful gardens which opened on to the waterfront. Later they moved to the Turner Company house with a 'fine well of spring water', abutting Spring Garden Lane. Apparently, Governor Bowring also stayed at the Turner property in 1854 when he became Hong Kong's fourth Governor.

Before arriving at the next point of interest, continue on past the 64-storey Hopewell Centre and the small shops selling rattan, glass, hardware, metal, etc. If you look closely, you can see shrines burning incense in these shops. It is these traditional practices in this busy, modern, steel and glass city which help you to appreciate Chinese culture.

Coming up on the left is the last stop on this walk, the **Hung Sheng (Sing) Temple** (11) at 129 – 31 Queen's Road East. The temple is built into the rocks and there are some huge boulders among the altars. Behind the temple is a superb banyan tree with long intertwined roots covering the rocky hillside.

The temple began as a shrine near the sea and in 1860, during the reign of the Ch'ing-Dynasty Emperor Hsien Fung, it took its present form. The site was sacred to fishermen who before sailing asked the blessing of Hung Sheng (Sing), a Tang-Dynasty scholar who became the patron saint of fishermen because of his ability to forecast the weather. He encouraged the study of mathematics, astronomy, and geography. One legend says he was reincarnated from the Sea Dragon of the Southern Seas, while another holds that he is the brother of Tin Hau, Goddess of the Sea.

On the left is the Golden Flower Buddha, who protects children and blesses their growth. To the right of the main god, Hung Sheng, are the 60-year-cycle figures, Tai Sui, or gods of the year. In this temple there are actually only 30 figures, with each one representing two years in the cycle.

The room to the far right is where the fortune tellers and palmists practise their art. There are two famous fortune tellers, one downstairs and the other upstairs. If you are interested in this ancient art, do not forget to make an appointment, and also bring along a Chinese friend who can interpret. In the downstairs room are Cheung Wong (the God who Picks Auspicious

Occasions), Shing Wong (Controller of Ghosts), and Kuan Yin (Goddess of Mercy).

This walk ends at the Hung Sheng Temple. You can return to Central either by taxi or by street tram.

Taxis are not allowed to stop where there is a yellow line drawn along the road, as there is on Queen's Road East, so walk to a side street or to Johnston Road (parallel to Queen's Road East).

The upper deck of a tram is a delightful way to travel in Hong Kong, so if you have not yet enjoyed this mode of transportation, now is your chance! (Refer to Kennedy Town Walk for a history of the tram, pages 24–5.)

To reach the tram stop, cross the street into Tai Wong Street West, a lane perpendicular to Queen's Road East. This lane is filled with shops selling birds, cages, and related paraphernalia. The first road you reach is **Johnston Road,** which was built on land reclaimed from the sea. In 1841 the shoreline ran between Queen's Road East and Johnston Road, thus making Johnston Road part of the harbour before reclamation.

Turn left and walk a few blocks to the tram stop and take the first tram going west into Central.

Bibliography

Arnold, John. *Hong Kong's Famous Funicular: The Peak Tramway 1888-1978* (Hong Kong: Peak Tramway Co, Ltd)

Burkhardt, V.R. *Chinese Creeds and Customs* (3 vols 1955-9) (Hong Kong: South China Morning Post, 1982)

Chamberlain, Jonathan. *Chinese Gods* (Hong Kong: Jonathan Chamberlain, 1983)

Clarke, Nora M. *The Governor's Daughter Takes the Veil* (Hong Kong: Canossian Missions Historic Archives, 1980)

Crisswell, Colin and Mike Watson. *The Royal Hong Kong Police 1841-1845* (Hong Kong: Macmillan Publishers H.K. Ltd, 1982)

Eitel, E.J. *Europe in China* (Hong Kong: Oxford University Press, 1983)

Endacott, G.B. *A History of Hong Kong,* Second edition (Hong Kong: Oxford University Press, 1973)

Evans, Dafydd Emrys. 'Chinatown in Hong Kong: The Beginnings of Taipingshan', *Journal of The Hong Kong Branch of the Royal Asiatic Society,* Vol 10, 1970, pp. 69-77

Government Information Services. *The Port of Hong Kong* (Hong Kong: A Government Publication)

Ho Fuk-cheung. 'Chinese Triad Societies: Classical Models and New Hong Kong Forms', *Hong Kong: the Interaction of Traditions and Life in the Towns* (Hong Kong: The Hong Kong Branch of the Royal Asiatic Society, 1975, p. 97)

Hong Kong Museum of Art. *Flagstaff House Museum of Tea Ware* (Hong Kong: Urban Council, 1984)

Hong Kong Museum of History. *History Around Us* (Hong Kong: Urban Council, 1984)

Hutcheon, Robin. *Wharf — The First Hundred Years 1886-1986* (Hong Kong: The Wharf (Holdg), Ltd, 1986)

Jarrett, V.H.G. 'Old Hong Kong' by 'Colonial' (Hong Kong: South China Morning Post, 17 June 1933 to 13 April 1935)

Jones, P.H.M. *Golden Guide to Hongkong and Macao* (Hong Kong: Far Eastern Economic Review Ltd, 1969)

Law, J. and Barbara Ward. *Chinese Festivals* (Hong Kong: South China Morning Post, 1982)

Lethbridge, Henry J. 'Caste, Class and Race in Hong Kong Before the Japanese Occupation', *Hong Kong: the Interaction of Traditions and Life in the Towns* (Hong Kong: The Hong Kong Branch of the Royal Asiatic Society, 1975, pp. 54-5)

Mattock, Katherine. *This is Hong Kong: The Story of Government House* (Hong Kong: Hong Kong Government Publication, 1978)

McLean, Robyn. *A Short History and Bye Laws of the Helena May* (Hong Kong: The Council of the Helena May, 1986)

Paterson, E.H. *A Hospital for Hong Kong. The Centenary History of The Alice Ho Miu Ling Nethersole Hospital* (Hong Kong: 1987)

Royal Asiatic Society Hong Kong Branch. *Hong Kong Going and Gone* (Hong Kong: The Hong Kong Branch of the Royal Asiatic Society, 1980)

Royal Asiatic Society Hong Kong Branch. 'Programme Notes for Visits to Older Parts of H.K. Island and to Kowloon, in 1974', *Chinese Tea Houses* (Hong Kong: The Hong Kong Branch of the Royal Asiatic Society, 1974, p. 218)

Savidge, Joyce. *This is Hong Kong: Temples* (Hong Kong: A Hong Kong Government Publication, 1977)

St John's Cathedral (Hong Kong: St John's Cathedral, 1976)

The First 50 Years 1911-1961 University of Hong Kong (Hong Kong: Hong Kong University Press, 1962)

The Royal Hong Kong Jockey Club Season 1986-87: A Brief History (Hong Kong: The Royal Hong Kong Jockey Club)

Topley, Marjorie and James Hayes. 'Notes on Temples and Shrines of Tai Ping Shan Street Area', *Some Traditional Chinese Ideas and Conceptions in Hong Kong Social Life Today* (Hong Kong: The Hong Kong Branch of the Royal Asiatic Society, 1967, pp. 123–43)

Williams, C.A.S. *Outlines of Chinese Symbolism and Art Motives* (New York: Dover Publications, 1976)

1A Communications Ltd. Tung Wah Today (Hong Kong: 1981/82 Board of Directors Tung Wah Group of Hospitals, 1981-2)

Index